CHEATED

Adina Rose Benedict

Mom,

lovely to meet you

Ax Ben

9-10-22

ISBN: 9798847429801

Acknowledgments

I would like to acknowledge the services of my editorial team AI Publishing, in particular Adam Lomond and Ian Melling

Special thanks to my graphic designer Robin Johnson who designed the cover of the book.
Contact details: RL Design, PO Box 19971, Jacksonville, FL, 32245
Https://gobookcoverdesign.com

Prologue

A story depicting the journey of the economic migration of families from the west sub-continent otherwise known as the West Indies who had come over to Europe in their masses in the mid 1950's in search of a new life and adventure. Many hoped to return after a short spell and having secured the finance to re-establish themselves. However, such was the draw of the western society that those harbouring the desire to return to their homeland had instead found themselves still rooted here, with perhaps no intention of ever returning. This fictional story seeks to illustrate how some families having emigrated to England can unwittingly find themselves perpetuating and fostering the traumatic aspects of their own upbringing, which are at odds with the new environment on to their children, often with destructive or damaging effects.

This fictional story set in the 1970's, depicts the story of one young lady whose life had been blighted from the daily rigours of family life, and who as a result feels she has been cheated out of enjoying a normal happy childhood, and subsequently must work hard to change the course of her life. Ultimately, this book charts the path Chastity takes in turning her life around from certain failure to one of fulfilment, success, and eventual marriage. Realizing that the tool of change lies within her own hands, she steers her life in the direction that she desires, building new relationships, rediscovering her giftings and her zest of life and above all, losing the archaic mantra which symbolized her parent's life, thereby allowing herself to enjoy life on her own terms.

Preface

Chastity Buchanan, one of four girls born to wealthy parents, was a bright vivacious child full of optimism and had defined determined goals for her life. But this soon changed, compounded further at the age of fourteen, when her eldest sister Diana with whom she had developed a very close bond with moved away to Bermuda to start a new life with her husband David. Whilst Chastity was happy for Diana, she felt bereft at what she saw as the loss of her sister, though at best, she knew Diana was only a phone call away.

Chastity's parents were born in Barbados and migrated to England in the 1960's, a few years before Chastity was born. Charles, her father, is a Professor of Mathematics while her mother Rebecca is a nurse. They have definitive ideas about child rearing and what they expect from their children and embraced and live within a rigid framework of values and moral concepts. They are members of the Christ Fellowship Group, a church that had its roots in Barbados, and an offshoot of the founding members had established a branch in Sussex. As we will discover, such a rigid lifestyle was to impinge on the development of Chastity as her life unfolds. As she grew up her parents began to force their views and opinions on her, eventually writing her off as she failed to live up to their expectations. Chastity went from a very confident and self-assured person to an individual who lost her zest for life, bowed down by low self-esteem and ventured on an involuntary journey into a wilderness

In a quest to win over her parent's love, Chastity began to do things that she felt would assure her of her parents love and hopefully enable her to find favour with her parents. In doing so, she took on a personality and identity which was an anathema to who she was and aspired to be. Such a deviation was certainly not of her own making. A classic case for mistaken identity of someone cheated from discovering their identity and developing meaningful relationships without the fear of being constantly judged by her achievements or failures.

But then Chastity hit forty and the need to take stock of her life dawned on her. What had she been doing with most of her life? What had she achieved? What were her milestones and was she enjoying the journey of life....?

Read on to find out how the story unravels.............

1

In The Beginning..........

Monday 5th of January 1975 was the first day at school for Chastity. Chatting excitedly to her younger sister, she felt all grown up as she started her first day at school.

'Chastity,' called out Rebecca, 'are you ready?'

'Coming......' Chastity squealed. It was a lovely morning; the skies were a sky shade of blue and the crisp autumn sun cast a warm glow in the hallway as Chastity put on her coat and her mother assisted with doing up the buttons. Mother and daughter took the short walk to the school, a Victorian style edifice surrounded by lots of greenery with a central building forming the focus of the square within the expanse of green which housed a beautiful statue of Martin Luther, a symbol of peace.

'Now you enjoy yourself sweetie,' said her mother and quickly embraced her as she watched Chastity walk up the steps and into the school building. This was to be her home for the next five or so years.

Chastity had been given the chance of going away to board at a school in Dorset but had declined as she was close to her mother and her eldest sister Diana and wanted to be at home with them. So instead chose to go the local private preparatory school. As a very grown-up child, confident, precocious and a born leader, Chastity had embarked on a new life which involved a new school, meeting and making new friends and becoming involved in new and wonderful challenges.

The first morning passed in a blur as Chastity tried to take in all the things she was being told as part of the initiation and enrolment procedure. By lunch time, Chastity had already made friends with Lucy, a white English girl, who apparently only lived five minutes away from her. Like Chastity, Lucy came from a middle-class background; her father, a company director, and her mother, a doctor, and so there were no supercilious notions about class and status. Lucy had openly embraced Chastity as her friend, but as time went on Chastity would see a different side to her.

'Come on Chastity, are you coming out to play? Lucy called out. In the playground they were playing a game of hide and seek.

'Do you have any sisters?' Lucy asked Chastity.

'I have two,' said Lucy. 'We are having a party at the weekend to celebrate my sister's birthday and I would like to invite you to come along.

'I'd love to come but I'll have to ask my parents first,' replied Chastity. Chastity is closer to her mother than she is with her father so she knew what the response of her father would be. Her father is very old fashioned and autocratic and harbours very strange views which usually extends to what friendships his children could or could not entertain. It would be a hard task for her father to agree for her to go, but Chastity thought she would ask anyway.

'Ding ding,' the school bell sounded in the distance. 'Right then children, pack everything away,' said Mrs. Hallam. As the end of the school day progressed, Chastity was looking forward to telling her mother all about it.

'Hello, dear,' Chastity's mother called out as Chastity ran to meet her. 'How was your day?'

'Oh Mother, school was such fun and I've made a new friend, her name is Lucy.'

'That's nice dear,' her mother said, 'perhaps you should invite her round for tea sometime.'

'Oh Mumsy, you know father wouldn't approve, he does not like us to have friends' round.' Even at that young age, Chastity was aware of her daddy's views, having experienced firsthand the way her older sister Diana fared when she tried to have friends' round for tea. And so, life at school continued.

Chastity's confidence grew as she became a popular girl and as she excelled in her studies, in particular English, the arts and sports, she was later made classroom monitor and enrolled in the school choir.

Three years later.....................................

July, the height of summer and the school term was ending. Chastity had been entered in for several events for the sports day and Mummy had promised to attend and had promised also to persuade Daddy to come too. Daddy did not normally care to appear at social school events. Such events passed by him in a blur as he only ever attended parent evenings, something in which he always had a vested interest.

Wednesday morning arrived as sunny and warm, like it had been all week. 'Goody, this is Sports Day,' Chastity yelled out! 'Mummy, don't forget you need to be at school at 2pm for the start of the games. Be sure to bring your kit, or better still, wear it as I want you to take part in the parents' race,' Chastity rattled on.........

'Okay dear, I'll make sure that we're there on time,' Mummy said.

'Oh, does that mean that Daddy will be coming too?' asked Chastity.

'Well,' Mum hesitated...... 'He has promised to try and leave work early so that he can attend. I've told him how much it would mean to you to have him there.'
'Oh goody,' exclaimed Chastity.

School had dragged on and Chastity had been distracted for most of the day but finally the moment had arrived. She had been practicing for most of the past fortnight and had managed to beat her best time of six minutes in the 800 metres. She was determined to win all the races for which she had been entered. Even at the age of eleven, Chastity was proving to be very competitive amongst her peers, particularly when it came to games.

The various classes were assembled with all the teams looking crisp in their neat sportswear; crisp white polo shirts with navy shorts for the boys and navy skirts for the girls. 'Come on, pay attention,' Mrs. Sangley said as she arranged the classes into their respective teams to start up the warm-up sessions. The atmosphere buzzed with excitement as girls giggled excitedly at each other and innocently teased the boys as they paraded around the field in their gear.

With the opening ceremony dispensed with, Ms Brahms the headmistress blew the all-important starter whistle and the games commenced. Ms Brahms opened with the usual introduction and goodwill for all teams. The first race, following the usual form is the egg and spoon race. This game was played by only the first three classes up to the second grade. Now for the older girls to show the younger grades what winning was all about. Chastity took to the stand for the relay race. Chastity had already won two races and the next race was the final race. They always left the relay race to the end; no-one ever knew why Chastity mused within herself. Perhaps it was because it was considered the race which epitomised the ethos and spirit of an event like this, where a display of team effort and comradeship was an invaluable component to the success of the games - and it was as if your whole year of success or otherwise could be summed up in this one race Chastity pondered. Chastity was very analytical and a deep-thinking person even at the tender age of eleven. Of course, Chastity won the race having decided beforehand that Lucy would run the last leg as she had a fast finishing time.

'Whooooooooooooooooooooooooo,' the girls screamed out when they realised that they had beaten their opposing teams to the finishing post. 'We've done it again,' Chastity shouted out, 'well done!'

'I have an announcement, pay attention everyone,' Ms Brahms said clearing her throat. It seemed too by the hoarseness of her voice that she had been actively involved in the cheering that could be heard on the playing fields. Ms Brahms seemed so prim and immaculate and a no-nonsense type of person, but it was rumoured that she had a mischievous side to her which on days like this, she allowed to surface.   'And now everybody, can we all pay attention,' she continued. 'We have reserved the very last race for the parents. Are there any willing parents here today?' This was always an amusing moment as parents jostled for position eager to be seen in the latest sportswear; women with coiffured immaculate hair, painted nails and made-up faces. The mums always outnumbered the men at these races. They included mothers who lunched, always noticeable in the crowd, working mums who had taken the afternoon off, and mums who had to be noticed in the latest naff designer gear, Chastity mused within herself.

'What was the point of all that dressing up when if they were going to win their respective race then they would have to run with all the gusto they could muster, and with every ounce of energy which they usually held in reserve for their much publicised gossip of what was going on in the village; who was dating who, and what the latest designs were in the shops and their recent holiday jaunts,' exclaimed Lucy who appeared to have read Chastity's thoughts so profoundly!

Chastity's mother had managed to get to the games on time and Chastity could see her as she approached the spot where Chastity, Lucy and a group of other friends had gathered.

'Hello Mummy, where's Daddy?' asked Chastity.

'Sorry, dear, he couldn't leave the office in time to attend. Never mind dear, I'm here - and look, they are asking for the parents so come along and support me, I hear you have already won two races, let's see if we can make that three, shall we?' Mummy was very competitive, and she always set out to win this race. She had also come well prepared in the latest trendy sports gear. She really did look the part, thought Chastity.

The headmistress blew the whistle, 'Ready, steady, go!' Mummy ran down the course sprinting quite fast, Chastity thought.

'Look at my mummy, go!' Chastity called out to Lucy, 'she's going at full speed..........!' screamed Chastity.

'Mummy, Daddy, come on…,' was all that could be heard as the chorus of voices rang out from the children, each of them egging on their respective parents to win the race. The first one to reach the winning post was of course Chastity's mummy.

'Well done, Mummy, you did well,' said Chastity, as her mother held aloft the gold medal she had won for winning the race.

'Phew, I'm not as fit as I thought I was, but I did it and here's another medal to add to the two you've already won,' Mummy said. 'Now all I need is a nice glass of Pimm's. Come on, let's head off home.'

'Chastity, Chastity,' Lucy called out, Chastity ran towards her. 'My parents are holding an end of term party come barbecue and I would love you to come. Let me know if you can. We're holding the party a week on Saturday.'

'I'll have to speak to Daddy first,' said Chastity, 'I'm sure Mum will be fine about it though.'

At home, Chastity thought of a way to convince Daddy to agree that she could accept Lucy's invitation. From what her mother had told her, her father Charles was so isolated from reality it was just so unreal. He appeared to live in a world where what he believed was the only thing that was right and proper and there was no room to entertain, consider, challenge, or even embrace any other opinion. He lived by his own moral code of conduct, and no-one would dare challenge him, as to do so could lead to heated arguments. Not even his own wife could challenge him. She was slowly becoming a shadow of her former self and she had begun to retreat within herself. This was quite an alarming sight to take in as Mrs. Rebecca Buchanan was by all accounts a vivacious woman, stunningly attractive with a zest for life, and a lady who cared deeply for her children and had the means to do the best for them.

'Hi Daddy,' Chastity called out, as she skipped along the hallway to be enveloped by one of Daddy's bear hugs. Sometimes, her father would be quite genial and not so austere and display what some might consider as normal behaviour. However, invariably, he could be quite moody and isolated, and you had to try and catch him when he was in a good mood if you were going to win him over. 'Daddy,' Chastity began tentatively, 'I've been invited to my friend's end of year party, please say I can go?'

'You know my position on going to parties. No, I cannot allow you to go because I don't know anything about them or their family,' Daddy said. Chastity knew what that meant. Her father had harboured these weird ideas that his children would be targets of some spiteful enchantment or maligned activity. Chastity's mother had told her that her father had been the victim of a very unhappy upbringing in that he was never allowed to socialize with his friends outside of the confines of school. His life had been peppered with a fastidious attitude towards rules and regulations, where it was a case of what you cannot do rather than what you could do. He never had the opportunity to integrate with other children outside the home for fear of being implanted with contrary perceptions and beliefs or succumbing to the ills of society. He in turn, though trying rigorously to resist such patterns of his father's behaviour, had instead unwittingly fostered them on to his own children.

Mother had sat down and had a 'heart to heart' talk with Chastity. 'You need to understand Daddy and why he appears to be so hard on you,' she began. 'He suffered some horrendous experiences as a child some of which he has not even discussed with me. It is a custom of Caribbean folklore that people can work bad spells on you which can affect your future and even the future of your own children and those of the generations that will follow you. It seems that everyone has a story about someone they know who had come under a spell from the dark world. Daddy therefore sometimes tried too hard and may appear overprotective of his family to the extent that he tries at all costs to avoid his family suffering in the same way he did. I have tried telling him that by being so stringent and rigid he inadvertently and not intentionally may cause his children irreparable damage and render them growing up with emotional problems and the inability to make and sustain friendships. I know you are still a child but a mature one at that. You understand, don't you?' Chastity nodded. Chastity and her mother sat there for a while and embraced each other closely.

After a while, Rebecca could see that Chastity was becoming quite sleepy and Rebecca left her to allow her to gently fall asleep. 'I wonder how much of what I said really registered with her,' Rebecca sighed to herself. Unbeknown to Rebecca, Chastity had digested every word that her mummy had spoken that evening; only time would tell how much and to what extent it would impact her.

2

Olivia Enters Centre Stage

It was ten days before the new term commenced and Olivia, Chastity's younger sister, was due to start school. Olivia was just as excited as Chastity had been when she first started at school. Olivia would be attending the same school as Chastity. But before all that, there was still one more week left of the holidays. The family had been planning an inclusive holiday to Marseilles in the South of France leaving behind the upkeep and maintenance of their home in the capable hands of the groundsman. He was a trusted worker who had worked for the family for several years.

The Buchanan's lived in Sussex in a large house which stood in its own grounds. The house spanned four floors with several rooms having en-suite bathrooms. There was a large oak beamed kitchen in which the family would often eat their evening meal; Daddy being a stickler for formal family insisted on formal eating arrangements at mealtimes. Towards the back there was a very large garden, more like a golf course because it was very large indeed! In fact, Daddy had a small golf course to one side of the garden, more like a mini golf course. They often held marquees in the summer and many a barbecue held in honour of the family's friends and colleagues. The Buchanan's were very fortunate and lived well.

The family spent their summers abroad and this year was no exception. They are a very close-knit family, and this was inevitable as they rarely socialized outside of the family unit and most of their friends were vetted by Daddy before they could pass the test of acceptability. As with all families, Chastity's parents had their favourite. They revelled in discussing and informing everyone about how gifted their son was who was a cellist and that he had won a prestigious place at the Royal College of Music. At the tender of age of twelve he had already won great acclaim and several awards for his outstanding performances. He was very shy though and self-deprecating. If you did not know him, you would not know that he was so gifted. As he progressed through life his fame and achievements did not change his character. He remained true to who he has always been; affable, a calming influence, passive and accommodating. He is a true gentleman.

Olivia on the other hand was a precocious child, bossy, academic and self-assured. Daddy and Mummy doted on her and could find no fault with her. She was the pretty one in the family with desirable fine English features, long loose curly hair, which had a sleeker look than Chastity's. However, for Chastity, her redeeming factor was that she was fairer in complexion to Olivia and throughout the trials of her childhood she used this to her advantage as a defence or coping mechanism against the somewhat unsettling events occurring at home. In non-Caucasian families, it was considered a great asset to be light skinned.

In the eyes of her parents, Olivia had it all and Chastity was soon to discover that the affection her parents had for Chastity was soon to be displaced by the birth of Olivia. Chastity was to witness the true extent of sibling rivalry at the highest level.

Rebecca busied herself with last minute packing. 'Come on girls let's finish the packing, we must leave in an hour.' There was a four-year gap between Chastity and Olivia, and so Olivia assumed the lead and took command. The girls were really excited about the impending trip. 'Olivia, let's see what's in your hand luggage. You might have to put some of your things with mine as you cannot possibly manage that case, it looks awfully heavy.'

'Mmm, I'm alright Mum, I'm taking my own things. I want to look after my own things.'

'Okay, well if you cannot manage your bags, remember I did volunteer to help you, but you are on your own now.'

'Well…………,' Olivia replied meekly, 'I may need your help a little.'

Diana, who Chastity was close to, had taken Chastity aside for a pep talk. Diana was seventeen and was attending college. She was studying for her 'A' levels. Diana had noticed that cracks had begun to appear in the relationship between Mummy, Daddy and Chastity, and she was becoming concerned. She knew her parents were inclined to be more favourable towards Olivia. They constantly made pleasant and complimentary remarks about Olivia but as regards Chastity, they just cast their eye over her as if she were unremarkable and insignificant. Diana knew that Chastity was beginning to feel isolated and wanted to assure that she was still there for her.

'We will spend some quality time together while we are away on holiday. We can go swimming and on long walks and do whatever you want to. As it happens it is our birthday (they shared the same birthday but were twelve years apart), while we are away, and we can celebrate away from the family if you like. I know Mummy and Daddy have plans to celebrate our birthdays while we are away, but we can also do something special together. How does that sound?' Diana said.

'Sounds like fun, I'll look forward to it.' Chastity said. And with that said, they both hugged.

Chastity loved birthdays as she got to spend time with her older sister whom she loved dearly. She never picked on her or belittled or tried to intimidate her. They would not always agree but there was a special bond between them that no-one dared to challenge, but also one which was not welcomed by their father.

'Chastity, here are some things that you might like to take with you. Here's a mirror, you're going to need that, plus some bits for your hair, and oh, take this lip gloss too! That should see you through the holiday.'

Diana was nice like that; she was always kind to me, mused Chastity.

Downstairs Daddy was packing the car. 'Can we bring down the cases now we need to get going?' Daddy called out. 'Dominic, give us a hand dear,' Daddy motioned to Dominic. Dominic was a tall teenager, well-mannered and liked by all. He was very popular at his public school where he was a boarder and Chastity was fond of him too and looked forward to the end of term as he was away at school and came home only at the end of each term. The family were now all ready to go.

It was an hour to the airport and Mr. Buchanan took his position in the driving seat of his range rover, one of his many cars (as he loved cars), as it had the extra room needed for all the luggage we were carrying. The car slowly pulled out of the driveway and Mr. Buchanan got out to close the gate and to have a last-minute word with the neighbour as he often did before we went away. He then closed the electronic gates and they were on their way.

Speeding down the motorway as they headed towards Gatwick, Chastity took out her mirror to ensure that her hair was in order. She hadn't liked the way Mummy had styled her hair and she wanted to check it over again. The mirror was ornately decorated and encased in a solid silver cover and with a long handle. It was a family heirloom but Mummy had allowed Diana to have it. Chastity held the mirror in her hand and admired herself in the glass, tugging her hair here and there to style it the way she wanted it to look. Chastity bellowed, 'Daddy, give me that mirror, I don't know what you want that for!'

The reflection is causing a distraction with my driving and anyway, it is not as if you can make yourself any prettier.'

'I'm just checking my hair,' Chastity said. There was a deathly silence as the others listened out to see if Daddy was going to insist and be difficult about something so trivial as a mirror. Daddy bellowed again.

'Chastity hand me that mirror, it is distracting me,' yelled her daddy. Daddy had never yelled at Chastity over something so trivial before and Chastity wondered what had upset him.

'Here,' Chastity said as she handed over the mirror expecting her daddy to put it in the glove compartment as according to him it was proving to be a distraction. But, instead, Daddy did the unthinkable. He smashed the mirror against the glove compartment remarking as he did so, 'There, you won't be using that mirror again. I don't want to encourage any of my children to become vain. Anyway, the book says vanity of vanities all is vanity,' retorted Daddy. Chastity watched as the mirror broke away into a zillion pieces of shards of glass.

'Oh...................,' Chastity exclaimed, trying to stifle a sob. Chastity was so shocked. She mumbled to herself, 'I wasn't being vain. How dare he, and then start spouting the Holy book at me.' Chastity thought a little and indignation rose within her. 'Anyway, I'm already beautiful - I wasn't trying to be something that I'm not.' Daddy did not respond. He just gave her one of those looks. Chastity knew what that meant. She felt crushed and did not utter another word until their arrival at Gatwick.

This incident had marred the start of the holiday somewhat and Chastity wondered what mood Daddy would be in later. She thought it best to stay out of his way until he had mellowed or thawed out a little. Chastity recalled this is something Diana would often do.

The flight was a short flight and they arrived at the airport in Marseilles and headed for the taxi rank. The journey to the hotel was a short taxi ride away and as they pulled up to the pathway in the taxi, the hotel looked just as beautiful as it did in the brochure they had meticulously peered over when booking the holiday.

'Here at last,' Mummy said and sighed a sigh of relief. 'Going away is so stressful, but now I'm going to unwind and enjoy myself,' she continued.

As they did away with the preliminaries and settled into their respective rooms, it was clear that every whim and need was catered for and this was usually indicative of the hallmarks of a good holiday.

It was the last night of the holiday and there was another family from England, the Fosters, who were on holiday too and over the week Chastity's parents had become quite chatty with them. Chastity and her sister Olivia had befriended their two daughters Charlotte and Emily, but Diana was much too old for them and had made friends with some other girls who were in her age group. But tonight, both families were going out for dinner along with Diana and her new friends. Charles was in a good mood. 'Let's do dinner in style tonight,' he said to Rebecca.

Both families were to dine at the exquisite restaurant The Versailles, a French restaurant in the heart of town. The restaurant was based within the Ritz hotel and was an acclaimed restaurant with three Michelin stars and they served a selection of foods including French and Italian and an array of desserts tantalizing enough to make your mouth water. One could easily opt for three courses of dessert and forgo ordering anything from the main meal. The Buchanan's and the Fosters were ready and gathered in the reception area of the hotel which was adorned in a very grand way. An infusion of traditional French architecture with Persian injected opulent furnishings graced the entrance to the hotel. The décor was on a very grand scale. In particular, the large lobby was decorated with the most exquisite materials from the fabrics of the curtains to painted leather panelled doors on either side. There were two marvellous large mirrors encased in elaborate silver frames behind the concierge desk and on the wall opposite and the centrepiece of this part of the lobby was a beautiful crystal chandelier. The Buchanan's did grandeur very well. They liked the finer things in life, and so for them this hotel had been the perfect choice.

'Shall we go then chaps?' Mr. Foster called out.

'Yes, we're ready and I can see the taxis are here too,' Charles replied. Charles being the perfect gentleman and a show-off too escorted his wife Rebecca, clasping his hand into hers and walked regally towards the taxi with the children following meekly behind. They arrived at the restaurant and Daddy formally introduced his children and his wife to the Fosters. They were shown to the table and sat down and began to eagerly read through the array of dishes on the menu. The diners had been handed menus both in French and English but Charles, eager to impress, showed that he was equally at home with speaking in French as he was in English. Rebecca, however, didn't care if she appeared to be a little vulnerable as she grappled with the language and chose to look through the English menu instead.

Charles couldn't help but launch into his usual pretentious mode, Chastity thought. He was good at that. Turning to Mr. Foster Charles started. 'This is Olivia my daughter. She's the same age as your daughter Stephanie. You know she's been accepted for the prestigious Notre Dame Grammar School to continue with her secondary education when she reaches secondary school age but we are considering sending her to the exclusive private Benendent School. You know they have a long waiting list, but parents are encouraged to put their child down on the waiting list from birth. You know the school is in the top five independent schools in the country.' Charles continued. 'Anyway, as I said,' Charles continued without stopping for breath. Olivia is very bright and is ahead of her years. It is such an asset to have a child so bright in the family.'

'Mmm yes, quite,' Mr. Foster said. He did not really know how to respond to that or even how to present a challenge to what Charles had just said. In fact, did he need to? 'My girls are also doing well at the local middle school. They are well grounded girls too and seem to be settled.'

Mrs. Foster then turned to Chastity. Chastity sat quietly tucking into her food while Charles and Mr. Foster continued with their conversation. 'How is school Chastity? I'm sure you must have lots of friends, you're a very pleasant and attractive young girl and shouldn't have a problem making friends,' Mrs. Foster said, her kind eyes twinkling as she spoke. But before Chastity could reply, her father butted in.

'Oh, you know when we get back from holiday Olivia will be starting at the school Chastity attends. I'm sure she will fit in with the structure and do well. Competition is always good for the soul isn't it'.

'Chastity dd..........,' Mrs. Foster interrupted. But Chastity just sat back in her chair. She knew her father and that he always had to have the last say in any conversation and that he would try to challenge anything that showed her in a good light.

3

Competitive Streak

The Buchanan's had arrived home after a fraught journey from the airport. It was the night before the start of the autumn term. Rebecca was busy ironing Olivia's uniform and getting everything ready for the next day. Olivia was with Chastity while they packed their school satchels ready with their new books and pencils. There was so much excitement that the air was tinged with it.

'Come on girls,' Rebecca called out to them. 'To bed please. I want you to be well rested for your day tomorrow.' Olivia could hardly sleep what with all the excitement and a little apprehension to boot.

'I hope you're sleeping Olivia?,' Mum called from outside Olivia's bedroom as she walked past on the landing.

'I can never fathom out how parents expect a reply if you're sleeping,' Chastity said aloud as she verbalized her thoughts. 'Surely if Olivia is asleep, she's not going to answer.'

'Shhh….,' her mother called out. 'You'll wake Olivia!'

The early morning sun shone through the window as dawn greeted the Buchanan household. The golden leaves on the trees glistened in the early morning sun as the dew kissed leaves hung limply. It was a picturesque day thought Chastity, just like my first day at school. Chastity felt all grown up as she had been given the responsibility of taking Olivia, her younger sister, to school. Rebecca busied herself with making the breakfast and summoned the family to the breakfast table.

'Now listen dear,' said Rebecca, turning to Chastity as she spoke. 'Be sure to look after your sister, show her around and make sure you're there with her during the lunch hour.'

'Yes Mummy, I'm quite capable, you don't need to fret or concern yourself. Anyway, the head of Olivia's year will take care of the initiation preliminaries – that's their job anyway but I'll look out for Olivia during her first week. She probably won't need me after the first day anyway.'

At school, Olivia revelled in the attention she was getting. 'Isn't your sister pretty?' Lucy whispered to Chastity. 'She seems such a happy child. She'll be a hit with the teachers.' Lucy continued.

'Yes, I suppose so, she is Daddy's pet!' Chastity replied.

The headmistress also appeared to be quite taken with Olivia. 'What a bright young child and so well mannered!' Mrs. Florence, the headmistress remarked.
'Yes Miss,' Chastity said meekly. She did not get the same attention when she had started school. What was all the fuss about, Chastity thought?

As time progressed it was clear that Olivia was indeed a bright child with everyone predicting that she had a bright future ahead of her. She excelled in the sciences and with precision, achieved top marks year after year in the end of term exams. She also enjoyed sport and competed at national levels proving that she was a good all-rounder. It seemed like nothing could go wrong for Olivia.

Time had moved on with Olivia completing her education at the prep school and then the independent middle school Bedales to take up her place at the grammar school. Meanwhile, Chastity had also moved on and was attending the all-girls private school, Trinity Manor. Her parents had chosen the school because of its position in the league table and because of its emphasis on music, a subject in which Chastity was keen to make progress in and pursue. The school had ranked first place in the school league table for all independent schools for five consecutive years. Both parents cared deeply for Olivia because she represented everything they could have wished for in a daughter and so it was at her mummy's insistence that Chastity was placed in a good school too also. It was mummy's desire that she should have the best for all her children.

4

Bereft and Alone

Diana, eldest child of the Buchanan family was all grown up - twenty-one years of age and no longer considered a child. She was no longer under Charles's jurisdiction but still lived at home. She was instrumental in maintaining the cohesion within the family and trying continually to stem or stamp out the sibling rivalry between Chastity and Olivia as they both fought for the affections of their parents.

Charles was becoming quite a bully - midlife crises it was thought, having recently just marginally failed to secure the Deanship at the university after a change in career whereas Rebecca no longer worked as there had been another two additions to the family. She now had a brood of five.

With the extension of the family brood, tension started to build up in the family home. Rebecca hadn't wanted any more children and the last two, Mary and Chloe were not planned - but abortion was never an option. It was not that they couldn't afford children, but the additions to the family meant that Rebecca would have to give up work. Furthermore, Charles was not quite ready to embrace the concept of being 'a hands on' father, as he considered his role to be that of main bread winner and any financial contribution that Rebecca made was a bonus.

The birth of Chloe was a difficult one. Rebecca had suffered two ectopic pregnancies prior to finally giving birth to a healthy girl who she named Chloe. The arrival of Chloe was with the usual fanfare of all the previous births. Aunts, uncles, cousins, and the all-important people, to Charles anyway, had descended on the family home to bring their gifts and express their well wishes. Rebecca was not really in the mood for entertaining and the birth of Chloe soon brought her into the despairs of post-natal depression. Cracks started to appear in their once seemingly perfect relationship with each partner wanting different things and not really listening to each other. It looked like they were growing apart.

One particularly cold January, Mother was really having a bad time of it and Daddy was in no mood to listen or to even take time to hear her out. He was having problems of his own, dealing with challenges at the university where he worked with the downsizing and restructuring of his department, plus there was the possibility that he might lose his job. Rebecca had been driven to periods of crying and going through emotional highs and lows. Chastity had discovered her in bed one afternoon; she was so shocked at her apparent state that she asked her daddy to come and see. Charles came into the bedroom and Rebecca was clearly not herself and Chloe had been in the same nappy that she had on the night before. She was not washed, and no-one knew if she had even been fed!

'Rebecca,' Charles said sternly, you're in a right state I think we need to call the doctor.'

'That's all you can say isn't it,' Mother shouted. 'What do you care, you're never here to help me anyway. All you do is provide the sperm and then tell me to get on with it. It would help if you got more involved with the raising of the children once they're born,' Mummy ranted on.

Daddy continued. 'Rebecca, I think you should calm down. Listen, I'll get you a cup of tea while we wait for the doctor,' he said, trying to remain calm.

'I don't want tea,' Mother yelled back. I need your support!'

'You don't know what you want,' Daddy answered back and then went quiet to quit fuelling the argument by shouting as he could see that the situation was in danger of getting out of control.

The doctor arrived, took one look at Rebecca and nodding sympathetically said out loud, 'Post-natal depression, the classic signs are quite apparent. She'll need to take some time out and I think it best if we arrange a short stay in hospital. We'll arrange for a social worker to call in on the family once a week just to make sure that you are all coping.' There was a long pause. Silence! No-one said anything for a while. There were glances being exchanged between the girls and daddy; the babies Chloe and Mary too young to understand, gurgled oblivious in their cots as the pattern of events were unfolding.

Mother had never been taken into hospital before and certainly not for depression. No longer able to keep her thoughts to herself, Chastity found her voice.

'I know she's not well, but she's not, not.......... not going mad,' Chastity shouted out staring at the doctor and looking him straight in the eye.

'No, she just needs some rest after all, she has had a challenging last year and she needs some time to recuperate. We'll do our best for her and don't you worry, we'll make sure that you have everything you need while she is in hospital.'

An ambulance was called and mother was taken to the hospital accompanied by Daddy. The girls stayed behind at home left with their thoughts for company and wondering if their mummy would be better soon.

Times were strained during their mother's absence away in hospital and Charles struggled somewhat to be positive and to find answers to why and how this could have happened. He never thought to look at himself. Perhaps he had not been as supportive as he could have been, but he never discussed his feelings with the children. He was too much of a mean spirited, stiff-necked, autocratic man to entertain the thought of discussing such problems with anyone else. No, it was down to him to sort it – he had to take control!

Meanwhile the girls were trying to cope, and it was obvious that they were missing their mummy. At school, Chastity confided in Lucy during the break session. Lucy just came out with it.

'You know what the problem is – it's your daddy. 'Your daddy,' she continued. 'From what you tell me he appears to isolate himself from the family unit. He needs to be more hands on and demonstrate less of the dictatorial style of fathering,' Lucy said quite authoritatively.

'That's very philosophical Lucy!' Chastity exclaimed, alarmed at the authority with which Lucy spoke, 'but I suppose you are right. He does not appear to be emotionally tuned in to us and what we're feeling and neither does he appear to be in tune with Mummy. He seems far removed from reality.'

With Mummy being away in hospital and the subsequent upheaval at home, the girls had to muck in with the household tasks. Aunty Claire, Rebecca's sister had been notified about what had happened and had invited herself over to their house.

One weekend as the girls were working away on the household chores, Aunty Claire, in her own ambivalent way, wrapped her arms around Chastity with that knowing look which said - I feel your pain.

'I know what you girls really need,' Aunty Claire said, 'a family outing. I'll take you away for the weekend, I'll just clear it with your father first.'

Charles had agreed that they could go, albeit reluctantly, as he did not want to give the impression that he wasn't coping. It was decided that they would go to Suffolk to spend the weekend with their auntie. This left Charles in the house to mull over his thoughts and work out a strategy to nurse Rebecca his wife back to full health.

Away in Suffolk and from the cares of life in the Buchanan household, the girls were really enjoying the freedom. The concerns of family life seemed so distant like it was someone else's problems and not their own. Laughing and enjoying the warm sea, they frolicked and basked in the warm sun, building sandcastles and playing 'spot the biggest jelly fish' with a prize being awarded to the one who won the challenge. Aunty Claire looked on proudly, then a frown came over her lined face as she grieved for the happy childhood that her nieces were being deprived of and which was far removed from the loving relationship and childhood she had enjoyed. She had chosen to shade under a large canopy in one of the many deck chairs dotted around the beach front. She then stood up and walking towards the girls, she began to ponder on what had gone wrong. Why had Charles her brother-in-law become so sullen - withdrawn almost and secluded, isolating himself from the very people who cared for him? If only he knew. She thought back to the time her sister Rebecca had started dating Charles when they were still in Barbados and how he seemed so interested in her, often just gazing at her - besotted almost, looking longingly into her face as he admired her fine features and the way her hair delicately framed her perfectly formed face. Rebecca was a pretty child of mixed parentage and had inherited the looks of her own mother who was an English lady and who had married a local man from Barbados very much against the wishes of her father, a staunch catholic. The pairing of the two of them caused so much uproar in the wider family that they didn't speak for years. Rebecca's family couldn't see what the problem was, but then looking back, colonialism was still very much in existence and mixed marriages of any kind were frowned upon. Furthermore, most of the countries colonized by the British were still in the grips of colonialism dogma and doctrine. But Rebecca, who was fiercely independent, knew her own mind and had even mapped out her own life in ten year spans, and in particular, highlighting the goals she needed to achieve and in what time frame. Aunt Claire reflected on how Rebecca, who was very popular at school, had excelled at nearly every subject, read widely, always dressed elegantly, and was almost a picture of perfection. Aunt Claire vowed within herself to try and had to help her recapture the joy she once had for life.

'Aaah...............Aaaaaah.' She was pulled back into reality at the sound of Chloe screeching as she tried pull her leg away from the clutches of what appeared to be a large jelly fish. Claire came running over from where she had been sitting, not even a stone's throw from where the girls had been playing.

'Oh girls,' she exclaimed quite crossly.' 'You need to pay more attention to your younger sisters. Look, Chloe has been bitten.'

Chastity and Olivia appeared quite crest fallen at the rebuke from their aunt but soon cheered up when they realized that it was only a small bite and superficial. Chloe didn't really seem to be too affected by it.

'Who's for ice cream?' asked Aunty Claire.

'Me, me, me,' the girls said in synchronized fashion. And with that, they raced towards the ice cream attendant to choose their trophies. Aunty Claire was kind like that. She may be cross with the girls for a minute if the occasion warranted, but her sternness never lasted too long.

5

A Bad Day at the Office

It was nearing the end of term and at the end of each term both Olivia's school and Chastity's school provided reports which charted the child's progress over the outgoing academic year. Chastity had somewhat fallen behind at school particularly in the subjects she disliked the most such as Geography, Mathematics and Chemistry and she was dreading what comments the teachers might have made about her. It was Wednesday afternoon and the last session of the day before half term. 'Now girls, remember we need to re-assemble with our respective form tutors to receive the end of term reports,' said Mrs. Macintosh who taught Chemistry. The girls filed out of the classroom to have their fifteen-minute break and Chastity met up with Lucy who had also joined them for break.

'Lucy!' Chastity called out, 'just one more chance to play a game of rounders - coming?'

'Why not, it is not like we are going to get much chance to see each other during the holidays, what with your parents behaving odd and peculiar about it unless we secretly arrange to meet up. We could do that, couldn't we?' Lucy said.

'Yes, yes, yes,' Chastity said, 'what a great idea!' Chastity and Lucy joined the boys Frederick, Gareth, and Solomon in playing rounders.

Chastity was quite fond of Frederick so too was Lucy and they would often joke about the possibility of dating him. Even at the age of fourteen both girls were socially aware and knew the rules of the game and could play it well to get the desired attention. 'What do you think - should we ask Frederick to meet up with us during the hols, or do you think he's got a girlfriend?' Lucy asked.

Chastity responded quickly, 'I'll be surprised if he hasn't - he's so dashingly handsome, what with that mop of blond curls that could sometimes do with a trim and which cascaded over his forehead obscuring his eyes. I love the way he would then toss his hair back in that alluring manner to speak to you or peer out at you from under his fringe. He was everything a girl could desire…with his piercing blue eyes - and a toned body which oozed with confidence.' Chastity went on like she was reading from a Jane Austen novel.

'Oh Chastity, gosh - hearken at you. What would your parents say, being so prudish. I doubt they would approve. If they could hear you now, they would perhaps think I'm a bad influence on you,' Lucy said. 'They may even stop you from associating with me because of the fear that I may lead you astray,' Lucy laughed, continuing.

'Oh, come now,' Chastity replied, sounding all grown up, 'they're not as prudish as you are implying after all, they had me,' though secretly, Chastity knew that her parents were so prudish and so pious that perhaps they believed they conceived her with their eyes closed and at arm's length!

Secretly, Chastity wished that her parents could be normal for a change so that she could have normal teenage conversations with them. 'Huh,' sighed Chastity, that was the bell and it was time to go back in for those dreaded school reports. 'Don't forget our plans Lucy,' she called out as she walked slowly back into the school building wondering what woeful fate lay before her.

Daddy made a big thing about reading out aloud the school reports and often would compare comments given by the respective teachers for Olivia and Chastity. So, Chastity was not looking forward at all to going home. She couldn't very well stay out as she knew that her father, with Mum being in hospital, was expecting her to be home that evening as she had not arranged any plans to do otherwise.

'Hi,' Chastity called out, as she threw down her satchel and placed her school report on the table in the study. Olivia was already home having finished at half day. 'Hi Olivia,' Chastity called out as she popped her head around the door leading into the lounge. 'Had a good day?'

'Yes,' replied Olivia, '..........and some good news too.'

'Enlighten me,' Chastity said.

'Well.......... I won first place in the School Public Speaking competition and look, my trophy is there on the mantelpiece.'

'I see,' said Chastity, admiring the golden figurine that stood proudly on the mantelpiece. 'Well done! Daddy will be proud,' Chastity replied adopting an older sister voice. Olivia is sure to be at the receiving end of daddy's affection and attention today and even more so that Mummy was still in hospital again. Chastity mused quietly within herself.

Mummy was still prone to bouts of depression and had again been admitted to hospital a second time, no doubt been brought on by the pressure and tension that was building up within in the family home. Chastity did not get the opportunities she once had to speak with Mummy and gone were the carefree days that Mummy enjoyed with her. Instead, Diana, her older sister had taken up the challenge of looking after her siblings while Mum was in hospital.

The key was heard in the front door. Charles had arrived home.

'Hello D-a-d-d-y,' screeched Olivia as she ran to greet him flicking her hair in a showy manner and at the same time intimating that she had something to show him. Daddy, astute as ever, sensed that Olivia had something to tell him.

'How's my little angel?' he said. 'And what surprise do you have for me today?'.

By this time Chastity had left the room and had gone upstairs to chat with Diana who was busy sorting out some clothes.
'Hi Di,' Chastity mumbled.

'Oh......,' Diana said hesitantly, 'what's wrong?'

'Daddy's being all affectionate with Olivia. Olivia is lapping up the attention and as usual I can't be bothered to hang around and play happy families. Anyway, what are you doing?'

'I'm sorting out some clothes because tomorrow Rupert and I are going to Wales for the day.' Rupert was Diana's boyfriend who she of course had kept hidden from her parents.

'Can I come?' Chastity asked. 'I would love you to come.'

'Not this time as we just want to spend some quality time together; perhaps another time,' Diana said, thinking to herself that it wouldn't be a good idea to have her younger sister hanging around her on a date, what would Rupert think? 'Anyway,' Diana continued. 'Daddy would have to know, and I couldn't possibly divulge the fact that I have a boyfriend. That would mess things up for us and I'm sure you wouldn't want that. No, we'll do something together, perhaps on Wednesday, or during the holidays. How does that sound?'

'Good…. I'll look forward to it. Can it just be the two of us as I think Daddy is taking Olivia to the Proms and then they're going out to dine with one of the professors at the university, and of course, he hasn't invited me,' Chastity rambled on.

'Fine, that's settled then,' Diana responded. Olivia enjoyed going out with Diana as it made her feel all grown up and she could talk to her about anything, especially about how she was feeling about Daddy. She seemed to understand.

It was Saturday morning; a nice feeling of spring in the air and Diana was going out with her boyfriend. Diana was a pretty lady with loose curls like her younger sister Olivia and had a smooth velvety chocolaty complexion. She looked a bit like Rebecca her mother but was of a darker complexion. Nevertheless, she was quite buxom and often drew admiringly glances from the guys in the neighbourhood. She sang beautifully and had a voice like an angel and was planning to be a singer, a notion to which Charles had surprisingly approved!

Chastity had got up early although she felt that she could have stayed in bed a little longer, but she wanted to make sure she had time to speak with Diana to wish her all the best for the day and perhaps give herself another opportunity to persuade Diana into letting her go with her.

'Bye everyone, see you later,' Diana called out. She had managed to explain quite convincingly to Charles that she was meeting a group of girls with whom she attended college, and they were all going on a geography trip and would be late back that evening.

'Bye see you later,' Olivia and Chastity responded in unison.

Daddy had got up and was in the kitchen preparing breakfast. 'We're going to see Mum today and when we get back, we'll look at the school reports,' he said.

He eyed Chastity with that look, and she knew instantly what that meant. Diana had gone out and so Chastity was all alone with no-one to confide in. She thought she had done well this year even though she had perhaps fallen behind a little in two subjects, but nonetheless, she hoped that the teachers had been kind to her.

At the hospital Mummy looked sad and a little dejected. Daddy was his normal brusque self. Olivia, being Daddy's favourite girl, managed to maintain her composure, but Chastity couldn't hold back. Daddy had stepped out of the room for a coffee and Olivia had pursued after him. Chastity had then taken this opportunity to speak to Rebecca alone and in private.

'Mummy, oh I really miss you. Daddy's so mean. When are you coming home?' Chastity blurted out as she sat on the bed next to Mummy.

'Listen dear, your Mummy is not well and she needs looking after. I may have to go away abroad and spend some time alone and try and get better,' replied Mummy.

'Oh Mummy, you're never going abroad and leave us with Daddy alone - you can't do that; we need you at home.'

Not one to vent her feelings or discuss her emotions openly, a bit like Daddy, Mummy listened silently as Chastity poured out her heart to her.

'Mummy, I feel like running away from home. Daddy's a bully. He keeps saying horrible things to me and he is being so terribly spiteful to me. He constantly pits me against Olivia and excludes me from most of the social functions he attends. I've been crying myself to sleep every night since you have been away in hospital. I can't even sleep some nights and I'm running away. I don't want to be at home anymore. With Dominic away at school and Diana always busy, I feel alone and very sad. Night times are the worse. It is like I go to bed at night and wish you were at home with me to give me a hug and assure me that all is okay. I'm tormented by images of Daddy goading me or making me feel small in front of Olivia and laughing at me which he does sometimes, just because in his eyes, I'm probably not living up to his expectations. He's so biased and doesn't care a hoot that he's too transparent about his true feelings about me. Oh................ Mummy, Mummy, Mummy!' Chastity sobs out loud................ 'You've got to help me!' And with that she ran into the bathroom to console herself as after all, what could Mummy do? Mummy needed help herself!

Chastity's mother sat there in the bed trying to digest everything her beautiful daughter had just told her. 'What was happening to her? How did it all go wrong?' she mumbled. It was inconceivable that her husband could be so mean she thought.

Daddy ventured back into the ward… 'Okay, dear?' He said as he motioned to Mummy. 'I hope you enjoy the chocolates I brought you. I understand that they will be discharging you on Saturday. Everything is fine at home. We're coping. Well you look better already,' he continued in a nonchalant manner.

Why did Charles have to be so functional about everything, so clinical? Rebecca mused. He never really knew how to be romantic or show convincingly that he cared about anything but himself and his precious career.

'Are they treating you well?' Charles continued.

'Charles,' Rebecca said, steering the conversation away from him. 'I need to have a private chat with you, do you mind?'

'Okay…………..' Charles said.

'No not here, in private……….' Rebecca said curtly.

'Very well then,' Charles said. They then went into the side room to talk.

'I wonder what that is all about,' Olivia said aloud to Chastity, 'Mummy sounded quite cross,' she continued.

'I wonder too,' replied Chastity fearing that Mummy might be asking Daddy for a divorce or be telling him that she wants to spend some time abroad, reflecting on the topic of the conversation she had earlier.

'Charles, I'm very concerned about Chastity. She does not seem happy. Is everything alright at home? Have you noticed anything unusual?' Rebecca said, giving Charles time to think before responding.

'Chastity's fine, if but a little distracted, but that's understandable bearing in mind that you are in hospital. Perhaps she is missing you. Yes, she appears to be distracted, which is understandable, but I'm dealing with that and have that in check.'

'Right, I see,' Rebecca responded. 'What exactly do you mean distracted?' she asked. 'You're not upsetting her, are you?'

'Don't worry yourself over such matters; concentrate on getting well,' Charles responded patronizingly. 'Anyway, as I said, I have the matter in hand.'

'Be gentle with her, she's a delicate soul, and it is me who will have to pick up the pieces later,' replied Rebecca.

'Anyway, we need to go now,' Charles said looking for a way to end the conversation. He wasn't going to be challenged by his sick wife, after all, he had everything in check and was in total control. 'We'll see you on Saturday and we'll prepare a sumptuous meal to welcome you back home.' And with that, he kissed Rebecca goodbye.

With a short parting embrace and with the girls ready to leave, they made their way out of the hospital. Mummy took a quick glance over her shoulder at the girls as they walked towards the exit praying that Chastity was going to be okay. She had been terribly moved by Chastity's outburst but did not know how best to deal with it. She could have had a frank discussion with Charles about her concerns, but this wasn't the time or the place. Or she could have spoken to Chastity about what was worrying her in more detail. Perhaps by Saturday she would have an answer.

6

A Display of Fortitude

Chastity was preparing lunch at home; Olivia had come in to help her. They were having smoked salmon with salad to be finished off with homemade lemonade and lemon sorbet. Daddy was having a coffee which Chastity had prepared for him.

Lunch was now ready to be served and because it was such a nice day, they decided to have it in the garden. Daddy had come out to join them. 'This is nice. Well done girls,' Charles remarked. 'Now where are those reports,' Charles said. Olivia, can you go and fetch them for me?' Olivia went into the study to get the reports while Chastity and Charles started on their lunch. Olivia returned with the school reports.

Charles read out a section of Olivia's report. 'Olivia, a bright intelligent girl, works hard and produces excellent work; predicted to achieve an A in her end of term exams. Keep up the good work,' Mrs. Holmes had written, who was Olivia's English teacher. 'Well, done Olivia - an excellent report,' Daddy proclaimed. You've done very well. Now, let's see how well Chastity has done.'

Chastity peered over her father's shoulder as he began reading her report. Charles read out a section of Chastity's report. 'Could do better but progress is impeded because she is easily distracted. Homework has been inconsistent which is regrettable as she has a lot of potential. I would encourage her to become more focused,' Mr. Humphrey her Maths teacher had written.

'This is disappointing Chastity,' Daddy said. 'I had hoped that after our pep talk last term there might have been an improvement in your Maths work. When are we going to see an improvement? Olivia is four years younger than you and her achievement levels far surpass yours - you need to start making improvements.'

'That's not fair Daddy, you know that Maths is not my subject and at best, I find the subject challenging. And it is unfair to compare and enforce competition in this way. If you read on, you will see that my English teacher has nothing but glowing comments to say about my progress. This should make you proud Daddy instead of nit picking on every negative detail,' Chastity blurted out.

Chastity was not prone to sudden outbursts, but she was becoming quite tired of what she perceived as Daddy's unreasonable criticisms.

'Go to your room, Chastity, I will not have you speak to me in that manner,' Charles retorted.

'But, but....... but..., I am,,,,,,,,,,,,,,,,,' Chastity started.
'No buts - to your room, now. I expect more from you, I am extremely disappointed!'

Chastity sobbed to herself. 'What was Daddy's problem. I will run away and then see what they do,' she mumbled to herself between sobs.

It is not like Olivia revelled in Daddy being horrible to Chastity, but she had to play the game to receive favours and privileges and continue scoring brownie points, so Olivia kept quiet. She was smart at doing things to please both her parents and she was always well rewarded. She knew what buttons to press and always knew what to say. One could say she was quite quick witted, even from an early stage whereas Chastity did not play mind games and only wanted equal treatment and fairness to prevail. Diana, her older sister, was such a confidant to her as she would retreat to Diana's room to seek comfort and some big sisterly attention.

It was late about 11.00pm and Olivia and Chastity had retired to bed. Daddy was downstairs in the study. He had decided to stay up and wait for Diana who had said she would be home at 10.30pm and she had not yet arrived home. 12.30am and still no sign of Diana and then at around 12:35am, the key was heard in the door. Diana let herself in and started walking stealthily up the stairs.

'Stop right there,' Daddy said raising his voice a little. And what time do you call this? I'm sure your geography trip did not take up the whole day and I recall distinctly that you said that you would be home by 10.30pm.'

'Hello, Daddy, we didn't finish working on the project until 7pm and then the train was delayed, and we had to wait for a reconnecting train,' Diana said without any reservation.

Clearing his throat, Charles hesitated and remarked. 'Why do I not believe you? I'm sure I saw your friend Caroline arriving by taxi half an hour ago. In fact, her mother called to speak with you, and I said that you had not arrived home yet. So where have you been then? Did Caroline go with you on this trip?' Charles was throwing question after question.

Diana was stung. Thinking to herself, she thought I must answer or give a reply. How should I respond? What if Daddy knows more than he is letting on? All these questions were running around in her mind. Her heart was pounding, and she could see that Daddy was not really in a talkative mood and she had to find a way to appease the situation. Meanwhile, Chastity had heard the commotion and had tiptoed onto the landing and was listening to the conversation.

Diana decided to play it straight and to be open and honest about where she had really been as after all, she was an adult and the worst thing that could happen is that she might be grounded. But at twenty-one, there wasn't much Daddy could do.

'Well, in fact I was totally honest with you about the agenda for today. I did go on a research trip for my geography assignment but there was just two of us that went on the trip. Rupert and I,' Diana said.
'And who is Rupert?' Daddy asked.

'Erm, erm………. Rupert is a friend of mine, we study together,' Diana said.

'What kind of friend. Is he a close friend? Are you involved with Rupert?' The questions were coming thick and fast from Daddy.

'To be frank Daddy, Rupert is my boyfriend!'

'Your boyfriend! Are you very involved, mmmm…………… erm……. erm………. Are you together………… you know what I mean?' There was a stunned silence. No-one said a word. 'Diana,' said Daddy trying to remain calm, I am very disappointed in you. You know my stance on boyfriends. I need to know plainly. Are you involved with Rupert on a sexual level?'

'No, I'm not,' Diana said. Our relationship has not progressed to that level yet.'

'I don't believe you,' Charles said. 'You spent all day with him today and you say that you study together regularly. It is not possible that you could remain untouched.'

'Untouched, what do you mean, untouched. What are you talking about Daddy?' Diana retorted.

'I mean sexually involved if you must!' Charles said. Daddy's voice had reached fever pitch by now and he was shouting.

'Daddy, you need to get with the programme and be clear about what you are saying. We're both adults and there is no need to pussy-foot around. I do understand such things after all, I am twenty-one years of age,' replied Diana.

Neither of them said anything for what seemed like ages. Then Daddy broke the silence speaking quite softly as he did so.

'Diana, it is late, and I think we should both go to bed, but there is one thing I need to say. While you are under this roof, I would ask you to adhere to my rules. You may be of age and feel that you are not under my jurisdiction any longer, but I forbid you from seeing Rupert and I require your undertaking that you agree to do so, and that from tonight that you will no longer continue to see him. I'm not about to embrace the concept of any of my children becoming pregnant out of wedlock, let alone engaged in some unsavoury activity.'

'You mean sex, Daddy,' Diana said. 'It is quite normal you know. But I'm a sensible adult and know what I want out of life. I'm not about to become a mother!'

'No, I won't hear of it,' Daddy retorted. 'I am asking you. I am not giving you an option. If you wish to remain living here in my home, then you must call Rupert in the morning and tell him that the relationship is off. I will speak to you in the morning.'

Diana walked up the stairs. Chastity grabbed her hand. 'Shh, not now Chastity. I'll speak to you in the morning,' Diana whispered.

'Alright, in the morning,' replied Chastity turning back to go into her room.

'You'd best go back to your room; Daddy's coming, I can hear his footsteps in the hallway,' Diana said.

Sunday morning. It was raining outside and there was a heavy atmosphere in the house. Chastity wondered why she felt so worried and then she remembered. Diana and Daddy had argued last night until the early hours of the morning. Oh, dear she thought, what is going to happen today. She went across the landing to Diana's room and knocked quietly on the door. Diana stirred.

'Is that Chastity?' Diana called out quietly.

'Yes, it is me, Chastity, can I come in?' Diana was sitting up in bed and let out a long yawn. It had been 2am before she had got to bed, and she was tired. 'What are you going to do?' Chastity asked. 'Have you given it much thought?' she continued.

'If you think that I'm going to allow Daddy to speak to me as if I am a child, you must be crazy. No, I am going to stand my ground and Rupert and I shall remain together.'

'Oh…….. what do you think Daddy will say once you've told him that you and Rupert intend to remain together?' Chastity said.

'I know exactly what Daddy is going to say, something like - you can't remain under my roof if you do not intend to abide by my rules.'

'He won't ask you to leave, do you think?' Chastity said.

'I don't know but if he does, I'll go!' Diana said.

'But you can't go, what about me, I need you! You know what it is like when Daddy gets into one of his moods!' Chastity said.

'Chastity, listen. I will always be here for you. I won't be that far away,' Diana said.

'Things won't be the same if you go away, what with Mummy spending long periods in the hospital, I'll be on my own,' Chastity said ruefully.

7

Diana Leaves the Family Home

Downstairs, Daddy was making the breakfast and Olivia and Chastity had joined him and Diana then came into the room.

'I've decided that I cannot agree to your demands and that Rupert and I want to continue with our relationship,' said Diana looking her Daddy straight in the eye. We're not doing anything wrong, and I don't see why we should not be friends.'

'Who's Rupert?' Olivia chirped in.

'Sorry Olivia,' Daddy said, 'Diana and I have something to talk about and she was out of line in discussing her shenanigans at the breakfast table. Can we go into the study please, Diana?'

'What's going on?' Olivia asked Chastity.

'Didn't you hear the argument last night?' Chastity asked.

'No, I was in a deep, deep, sleep,' Olivia replied.

'I need to brief you then,' Chastity said. 'Yesterday, Diana came home late, 12.35am in fact, and they had an argument. I was listening at the top of the stairs. She revealed that she has a boyfriend, Rupert. Daddy was livid and said that he could not allow her to remain living here at the house if Diana continues with the relationship. I spoke to Diana this morning and she said that she was not going to end the relationship with Rupert.'

'Oh no!' Olivia exclaimed. 'I hope Daddy doesn't ask her to leave. We really need her around here, what with Mummy in hospital all the time.'

Diana walked back into the dining room. 'I'm leaving girls, Daddy has asked me to leave, but I'll keep in touch with you both.'

'No.......................... you can't leave,' sobbed Chastity. 'Daddy, please say she can stay.'

'Diana is not prepared to end her relationship with Rupert, and I'm concerned about the effect that her shenanigans will have on the rest of you girls, especially Olivia,' Daddy said.

Diana went upstairs to pack. She packed as much as she could in one of the larger suitcases and then called a taxi.

'Where will you go?' Chastity asked her.

'I don't know, I'll give Rupert a call and see if I can come over. Here, take my pager number and keep in touch,' Diana replied, passing Chastity a crumpled bit of paper with her number scribbled on it.

Diana kissed and embraced the girls and said her goodbyes.

The same day that Diana left, Dominic was away at school but was due home for the holidays once the Speech Day service had ended which was usually around at 5pm. Her youngest siblings, Mary and Chloe being just one and two years old respectively were asleep in their cots upstairs and her Mummy was due home the same day. The situation couldn't be worse but none of this concerned their father. He had made his decision, and nothing was going to cause him to change his mind. In fact, in his eyes, Diana had decided her own fate in not agreeing to end her relationship with Rupert.

Charles left to collect Rebecca from the hospital. Reflecting on the events of that morning, Charles thought, goodness knows what she will make of his decision to ask Diana to leave. One thing's for sure, when he decided on something, he did not see why he had to get his wife's approval before instigating his decision.

Arriving at the hospital, Charles had decided to fake how he was feeling a little and greeted his wife with a cheery voice.

'Hello dear, nice to see you. How are you feeling?' Charles said. 'I have something to tell you. Diana has decided to leave the family home. We had a disagreement yesterday and she wouldn't agree to comply with what I had asked her to do. There is nothing more to be said and I decided that it was best for her to leave.'

'What do you mean she has left home? I know she is of age and perhaps wants to rent her own flat, but I have not seen her for weeks, and we haven't even had a chance to say goodbye,' Rebecca responded.

'I'm sure she'll keep in touch with you and anyway, she has a boyfriend, and I don't want her imposing her decadent lifestyle on the other children. It would be impossible to keep order in the house with Diana flaunting the house rules. You know what she is like; so strong headed and petulant and this may have a negative influence on the girls. Also, with Chastity under performing at school now she does not need any further distractions,' said Charles in a matter-of-fact kind of way.

'You shouldn't be so hard on her. She is an independent responsible woman,' Rebecca said.

'Well, she can go and be independent elsewhere but not in my house,' Charles retorted.

'It is not your house. It is our house, and I should have a say in what goes on in our house,' challenged Rebecca.

'You mustn't worry your little head over everything. You'll see that my decision is in the best interests of us all,' Charles retorted.

'Have you broken the news to the rest of the family?' Rebecca asked.

'The girls know of my decision, but Dominic is yet to be informed. I'm picking him up from school tomorrow. We'll go together and you can break the news to him,' Charles said.

'That's not fair, you should do as it is your decision and there is no way I can back you up on this one,' Rebecca yelled at Charles.

'Okay, okay, I'll speak to Dominic!' Charles retorted.

They walked to the car and drove the short journey home. The girls were babysitting and watching television. Supper had not been prepared and so Charles and Rebecca suggested they order a takeaway. Rebecca thought that it was important to start building bridges and to continue with family life as normal if they were to prevent a massive fall out to Charles decision. It was more so than ever before to keep the channels of communication open, but this was going to be difficult with Chastity being so vulnerable as she had taken Diana's departure quite badly.

Diana had left a gaping hole in Chastity's life. Diana had left home and Chastity was bereft, her one confidante gone forever. Chastity felt cheated now that she had lost her best friend and unloved, like no-one really cared about her or what she felt and there was no-one there for her. Diana was, and indeed, had been her best friend. As her older sister, they had gone on trips together and seemed to have so much in common although there was over fifteen years between them. They spent birthdays together, discussed their dreams and hopes together, and planned their futures together. Everything looked rosy until this fateful day.

Since Diana's departure, events had already started to take a turn for the worse. Chastity had become quite poorly and was advised by her school counsellor to take time off from school. Such was the frequency of her absence from school because of her being sick all the time that Mummy decided to take her to the doctors. The family doctor, Doctor Roddick, was a lovely person and a well-respected doctor by most standards. Chastity had lost a lot of weight and it was feared she may be suffering with anorexia nervosa. She would eat at family mealtimes, but she didn't seem to be maintaining her weight and looked very thin and quite gaunt. Her hair lacked lustre and she was not her usual buoyant self, not that she had much to smile about recently.

At the doctor's surgery, Rebecca presented Doctor Roddick with a health synopsis on Chastity.

'Doctor, I think my daughter is showing signs of anorexia. She has lost a lot of weight recently and although she complains of stomach pains she has been known to be incessantly vomiting especially at school. Last week her headmistress sent her home because she was so weak that she was unable to continue with lessons.'

'Can you tell me how you are feeling?' Doctor Roddick said, turning to speak to Chastity.

Just the sound of his smooth mellow tones made Chastity feel weepy and emotional. She felt like crying but managed to compose herself.

'I feel so empty inside that I don't know who I am anymore. I feel like my identity, the person, the real me is being eroded away. I've lost all confidence. ....'

'Chastity....' The doctor said pressingly, 'what physical symptoms are you experiencing?'

'I am having tummy pains and I feel sick all the time. I feel tired all the time and have little energy,' Chastity said.

Doctor Roddick paused as if he was trying to assess the condition of his patient.

'Mmmmmm,' he said. 'We'll arrange for you to undergo some tests and then we'll see what the results yield. In the meantime, I will arrange for you to speak to the school counsellor. I will also prescribe something for the nausea and we will continue to monitor the situation.'

'How are Mary and Chloe, and how are you now since your discharge from hospital?' the doctor asked turning directly to speak to Rebecca.

'I am much better, but any relief is short lived as my concern is for Chastity as she does not appear to be herself. She used to be so vivacious and confident and was making good progress at school, but now her schoolwork is suffering too!'

Pausing a little to gather his thoughts, the doctor replied, 'perhaps we should arrange for Chastity to see an educational psychologist, but I think we'll wait to see the assessment from the counsellor first.'

Another social worker was appointed to the family who was assigned the task of looking after Chastity. Her name was Connie. Chastity liked Connie instantly and believed she had found a new friend in Connie. She was not a replacement for Diana her older sister, but she was a substitute. Connie encouraged Chastity to talk about her feelings and to telephone her whenever she needed to talk. Charles was not keen that Chastity needed the support of a social worker and often accused her of pretending to be ill to get attention. He referred to her sickness as the 'phantom.' There was no sympathy for Chastity from her father not that she really expected it.

It would be very difficult for Chastity to maintain any meaningful contact with Connie as the phone was not permitted to be used for anything other than necessary calls. Chastity pondered whether any calls to Connie would be considered as necessary in the eyes of her Daddy.

With the passage of time, things in the Buchanan household didn't really get much better.

A year or so had passed and as if to add insult to injury, Charles had forbidden any of the family to keep contact with Diana as he seemed to believe that she was a bad omen, leaving the family home under such a cloud. It was inconceivable to Daddy to think Diana could bring anything positive into the family unit if she was living a life of decadence. But contrary to what Charles believed, Diana was now happily married and living in Bermuda. She had married a wealthy diplomat and was enjoying what most would consider as the high life. She had written a letter to Chastity giving her all the details and sending her the necessary contact details. The letter arrived one Saturday morning. The night before, Rebecca and Charles had gone to bed rather late and it was suggested that perhaps the older girls, Olivia and Chastity, would make breakfast for Mummy and Daddy in the morning.

'That's a stroke of luck,' Chastity said reflecting on last night's conversation, because if Daddy or Mummy had been up earlier, they might have got to the post first. But as it happens, I've got there first. Look Olivia, a letter from Bermuda from Diana. She's emigrated to Bermuda; would you believe it!' she shrieked.

'Shh………. they'll hear you,' Olivia said, referring to their parents. 'Pass it over let's see.' There it was, plain for everyone to see, a letter from Diana. 'She hasn't forgotten us then,' remarked Olivia. 'What are you going to do? Are you going to respond and write back; you know what Daddy said!' Olivia continued.

'Who cares what Daddy said, I know Mummy would be very happy to know that Diana is doing well. She's still my sister and nothing will ever change that,' Chastity said.

Chastity decided that she was going to maintain contact with Diana, but she did not confirm her decision with Olivia just in case Olivia decided that she could not keep this a secret from Daddy. Mummy of course would be okay with this, but then again, she did not have much say in the matter as Daddy had eroded away at her self-esteem to the extent that she was no longer able to voice her opinion on anything. War had broken out in the Buchanan home and the casualties of war were Chastity and her mother Rebecca.

8

Odd One Out

Back at school, Chastity was making some progress but had days when things just seemed so dark and bleak. She was excelling in her English studies but she was gradually becoming withdrawn and this was affecting her ability to socialize with her peers and establish friendships. The true extent of this could be seen particularly in physical education lessons, a subject which she detested!

Physical education lessons were timetabled for the summer term to take place on Thursdays. Chastity was wondering how she would get out of participating in the class. Last week she had self-penned her own note and had got her mother to sign it saying that she was having her monthly cycle that week and therefore felt unwell to take part in the class. Her mother had signed it. Chastity did this often and she had so far successfully managed to be excused from the class. But this was a new week, and she could not use the same excuse twice. Mrs. Adams would never fall for it.

'Oh dear,' thought Chastity, 'I so don't want to do PE this week.' But try as she might, she could not think of an excuse that was convincing enough to use. She had had her cycle, she didn't have a cold or the flu, and she did not have hay fever. 'But.......... I could always say I had leg cramps, Miss might buy that excuse,' Chastity thought. So, armed with her satchel and her PE bag she boarded the bus to school.

3pm and Class 3A had assembled in the gymnasium. Mrs. Adams, the physical education mistress in her usual brusque voice made the announcement that today they would be teaming up for netball. On hearing this announcement, Chastity's mind went into overdrive. Thinking to herself of a way to get out of the class, Chastity muttered under her breath, 'I hate netball and I need so badly to get out of this session.'

'Miss, I am not feeling well, I have cramps in my legs and can I be excused from PE today?' Chastity asked.

'Chastity, if it is not a headache, or a sore tummy, you always have another excuse. I think a little exercise might do you a world of good and I would like you to participate. In fact, I am asking that you participate in games today,' Mrs. Adams replied.

So that was it - there was no getting out of class this time, Chastity thought.

The usual practice when netball was on the agenda would be that the class would be divided into two teams, and they would play against each other. Mrs. Adams took charge and nominated Stacy and Vanessa to choose their teams. There was as usual a lot of sniggering going on because there were a few girls who no-one really wanted in their team and these girls invariably would be left to the end. It would then be down to Mrs. Adams to step in and allocate the remaining girls to each of the main teams.

Chastity had drawn the short straw and this year she had not been scheduled to do games at the same time as Lucy, simply because she had chosen different options in year 10. If previous experiences were anything to go by, Chastity knew that she would be one of the girls who would not be chosen. But she desperately, surreptitiously even, hoped that someone might pick her. She sat on the bench while the team leaders set about picking their team.

Stacy started first. 'I'll have Caroline, I'll have Bethena,' Stacy began. And so on. Then it was the turn of Vanessa to choose her team.

'I'll have Ruth, Lizzy, Caroline,' and one by one, Vanessa set about choosing her team players.

And so they continued choosing their teams until there was only three girls remaining. These were Chastity, Stephanie and Hazel. If Chastity was the confident person she was when she first started out at the school, she would have no problem fitting in and perhaps would be the one that would have been selected to pick the team.

9

Counselling

Attendance at the private clinic became a permanent fixture this being one of the main ways Chastity could voice her concerns and get the attention she needed. So too was the increasing feeling of social exclusion with her father insisting she keep her friends as school friends only and discouraged her from extending those relationships outside of the confines of school. The only way she could console herself was by crying herself to sleep, something she did often.

It is not like her peers at school did not try and foster and forge friendships with her, but that her father was always trying to live his life through Chastity and his other children. Such weird patterns of behaviour infringed on Chastity's ability to make friends and to maintain those friendships, and which eventually led to Chastity developing and somewhat accepting a poor self-image of herself.

Since the departure of Diana, Chastity often resorted to recording her innermost feelings to her diary. At least no-one could read them and anyway, she kept the diary hidden under her mattress. If her father found out he'd be terribly angry as he was becoming so paranoid.

November 23 .... She wrote..........

'Diana leaving the family home abruptly - my soul mate gone forever and left me alone to face Daddy. Apparently, Daddy had said she had done something which he did not approve of, and while she lived under his roof she had to abide by his wishes. Diana, now a young woman, thought differently and because she saw herself as a well-meaning person and disciplined in her lifestyle, how she chose to live her life shouldn't have posed a threat to Daddy and his way of life. Daddy has said something about trying to keep the rest of the family from what he considered to be a decadent lifestyle and needed to encourage us (bullying - more like it!!!!!) to study hard and embrace a very disciplined lifestyle.'

'Parents evening last week. Daddy bragging on about how well Olivia had done. Nothing positive said about me. I might as well be invisible.'

'School reports being compared again. Can't take much more of it! Oh, to be a bird then I could fly away and leave all this behind. Daddy never takes me out anywhere important. Always takes Olivia with him on important functions.'

December 26

'I attended the Dorchester Hotel yesterday, only because Olivia had another engagement to go to. He must despise me - always says I'm stupid; someone going nowhere fast and will never amount to anything. But I can challenge that as I found out he never got a 1st in his mathematics degree, a 2:2 more like it!'

'Mummy had become ill again - constantly in and out of hospital as a direct result of the stress at home.'

'Daddy is so mean; crying myself to sleep; my favourite brother away and no one to console me. 'I'm going to run away, but how and where to?'

10

All Alone

Chastity committed more thoughts to her personal diary.

15 February.......... There is one king in the family home, his word being sacrosanct and as a man's home serves as his castle, this is what Charles had decided. It was becoming clear that he despised women who were independent and assertive and who liked to take control of their own destinies. It was like he thought he had been put on planet Earth to rule the world and stand up for the male race as if it were a dying breed. He certainly did not want Chloe, Olivia or even Chastity turning out the way Diana had. He had to protect them, control the way we thought, make decisions even relating to the person we married – or so he thought. Well, he tried very hard to enforce this mantra.

Chastity reflected on how the absence of Diana was still being felt especially by Olivia and her mother. How could a father so cruelly move his own daughter out of the family home without as much of a goodbye? Despite all the protestations made by her well-intentioned friends and indeed by Diana herself, it was clear that Charles was not one for turning.

With Diana gone, Chastity was miserable. Diana was the one person she could have counted on; the one person who could console her when it seemed the whole world had ganged up against her. Her mother tried her best or so it would seem, but even when she needed support her frail state of mind meant that to keep the peace she would stay out of any confrontation.

But Chastity was not prepared for the path that lay ahead of her. She had hoped to draw comfort from her sisters Olivia and Chloe though Chloe was only eight years old.

Olivia had mentioned to her how much of a calming influence Diana had within the family. Chastity was surprised at the conversation with Olivia. She could now see that it appeared like she was not the only one feeling the absence of Diana as she was up to the point of her departure, the one constant force for stability in a house of emotional unrest. It wasn't surprising though, as being the eldest of the Buchanan's children, Diana would naturally have a wiser head on her shoulders. She was someone who one could turn to for advice on a myriad of things and other matters of the heart. She was not so much of an academic, but she was a good person to have around. She had helped to bring calm to a home environment which would often become fraught with contention when Mummy and Daddy were letting off steam.

It was becoming increasingly apparent to Chastity that Olivia and Chloe were becoming close. This often meant excluding Chastity from many things that they may have chosen to do together. Olivia was twelve and Chloe nine so they didn't attend the same school, but Chloe envied the relationship that Olivia had with Daddy and aspired to be on an even keel with Olivia. She therefore did everything in her power to cultivate the same kind of rapport and closeness that Olivia had with Daddy.

Summer holidays were the worse. A paradoxical time of relief; school was out but there loomed invariably also a foreboding cloud of contention because Chastity knew that with Diana no longer at home, she would have no-one to pair up with. It always fell to her to somewhat assume the role of helper which would invariably mean helping her parents out with various tasks and ensuring that everything around the house was as prepared as it could be.

During the summer recess, and the busyness of it all, there were moments where Chastity could find some solace and for a moment forget about the troubles in her life.

Chastity loved the long drives especially if they were going down to Dorset or Cornwall which they often did at the beginning of the summer holidays and then finished off with one or two weeks abroad in the South of France. This time however, the family were planning a vacation to Greece and were going to spend a few days in Bermuda and then move on to The Bahamas for some serious sightseeing. As a family, they all were looking forward to going away.

'Chastity,' Mother called, 'come on dear, give us a hand with the packing.'

Mummy liked to take a few home comforts when travelling abroad; things like cereal and bath time stuff; also, the essential condiments like herbal infusions and the espresso coffee from Waitrose which Charles loved. With the packing done, Chastity made her way over to help her younger sisters, but they pushed her away, they didn't like her hanging around.

'Thank you, Chastity, but we can manage thank you,' Olivia said.

'That is fine by me, I'll leave you to get on with it,' Chastity responded.

It always appeared to Chastity that any offer of help was clearly not welcomed, and that Olivia and Chloe appeared to intentionally isolate themselves from her. Chastity was sure she was not being paranoid, and she thought that there was one way she could play them at their own game and that was not to allow them to see that their behaviour was upsetting her. Anyway, Chastity thought, I'll block out all that nonsense. It is going to be a fabulous holiday and there will also be a grand birthday party for Mummy who was turning fifty. Parties were a rarity in the Buchanan household but on one this occasion, Charles had relented and had been only too pleased to arrange a birthday party for his wife. His view was that parties were self-serving affairs and that they were something that he could do without. He could afford to have a birthday party for every one of his children, but he was a miser and things like money were never discussed.

It was a beautiful sunny day as they arrived in Greece as the early morning sun greeted them as they arrived at the airport in Athens. The sun kissed palm trees swayed in the gentle breeze whilst the blue skies appeared to join in with the melody. 'Beautiful,' sighed Mummy as she sniffed in the balmy air and gathered Chloe her youngest under her protective wing. Chloe tried to pull away.

'I'm alright Mum if a bit tired,' but secretly Chloe wanted to pull away and go off with Olivia.

They arrived at the hotel and Mummy took charge straight away.

'Olivia and Chloe will share one same room and I've arranged for Chastity to have her own room, and of course Dominic will have his own room too. Shall we say we'll meet up in about two hours to give you time to take a rest and then we'll discuss the itinerary for the day,' Mummy said in soft punctuated tones. Chastity was often overprotective of her mother as she hated to see her constantly at war with Daddy. Mummy however was of the old school era, never really allowing herself to burden Chastity with wifey troubles and believed in keeping a separation between domestic affairs and her children's involvement in the same. However, she was slowly changing tack as Chastity seemed to have a mature head and provided an avenue for her to offload some of the stress. In the main, Chastity was looking forward to the change of scenery the holiday would provide and exploring the surroundings but most of all, getting away from the all-encompassing home life and the ill treatment she was often subjected to her by her younger siblings. Yes, her siblings often bullied her but when challenged they would say they were only having fun. But fun at Chastity's expense is the way Chastity perceived it. It would be okay if it was harmless, but oftentimes it was personal and it was like her father had cloned miniatures of himself to provide some macabre back-up for his systematic ill treatment of Chastity. Chastity would often be the subject of snide comments by her younger siblings who could often be found whispering together whenever Chastity walked past their room or passed on the landing on the upper floor or anywhere in the house. On one occasion, it got so bad that Chastity could not help herself or hold back her feelings of resentment towards being treated in this manner.

On one day, it became so bad, Chastity just let rip. 'Oi, what is it with you two? For God's sake grow up – why are you being so mean? It is not like I'm mean towards you.' After that outburst, it seemed like this was what was needed to put a stop to this silly behaviour. After this the girls were slightly more behaved in a more civilized manner, if just a little.

Generally, Chastity so badly wanted to be included in their cosy relationship she would ask if she could join them if they were going out anywhere. On one such day she plucked up the courage to ask. Plucked up the courage – it sounded strange when she was the older sister but that is how they made her feel – worthless, inferior and something that you would find at the bottom of their shoe!

Olivia was going out to the library – or so they told Daddy and taking Chloe with her. 'I need to go to the library. Daddy said you were going out, why don't we go together we can perhaps stop for coffee on the way?' Chastity gestured.

'Oh, we're not going again. We're just going for a walk to the park to just chill out,' Olivia said.

'OK then, we'll go some other time then,' Chastity volunteered.

At the library Chastity heard a familiar laugh 'Oh that sounds like..................,' Chastity thought, 'like Chloe,' Chastity said out loud. She peered around the column which divided the reference section of the library from the photocopier machine and microfilm machine. 'Oh, Chloe............Olivia what....... You said you weren't going to the library and that you had changed your plans for the day,' Chastity exclaimed!'

'Oh, we just had a change of plan,' Olivia responded.

'But.........you could have said,' Chastity said. On reflection it was typical of Olivia to play games of this sort; secretly going off and pretending to cancel plans which involved her at very short notice. Chloe was quite mean spirited to Chastity and although Chloe was the youngest child, she often ran rings around Olivia. She had that much influence even at such a young age. Olivia and Chloe had bonded well and one could see a pattern emerging. Olivia and Chloe were bonding together with Chastity becoming increasingly isolated. With Mum increasingly away in hospital, Olivia had become a surrogate mother to Chloe. Olivia became confidante, counsellor, mentor, and teacher to Chloe. There wasn't room within the cosy friendship for anyone else and that included Chastity. They even shared secrets together and banded together against Chastity. If they weren't sisters, one could be forgiven for thinking that they were a couple. No-one, not even Mummy could see the dangers looming with such a close knit, unhealthy friendship developing, and Daddy, well, he didn't care anyway. He despised Chastity and didn't care enough that such an experience would affect and impact upon her as a young woman perhaps well into her adulthood to the point of affecting her ability to establish meaningful friends. For Chastity, there was no-one absolutely no-one. Her mother found this hard to grapple with as she had showed so much courage and potential. What had Charles done to the family home? It was like he didn't care – stubborn, autocratic and caught up in his own thoughts. His world revolved around him and his work only and of course Olivia. Olivia and Chloe had both found solace, security and self-worth in each other and Olivia, comfortable in the knowledge that she had found great favour and was able to exert considerable influence by being Daddy's favourite girl. She revelled in it and Chloe felt secure in knowing that she was being nurtured by Olivia, if not by Mum, who always appeared to be emotionally distraught and wrapped in a cocoon of self-pity unable to embrace the needs of her family. Her family needed her right now, but it was becoming increasingly evident that she was not coping.

Chastity continued to seek solace in her diary, and it was her diary she would turn to when she was down, recording notes of pages and pages of what was happening at home. She harboured thoughts and ideas of how she might get the attention of her persecutors but had thought there was little to be gained as things looked too far beyond repair to change. On one occasion, Charles had got wind that Chastity had been keeping a diary. He had found her hiding it away under the mattress of her bed. He went ballistic. 'What is this?' he demanded to know. Chastity had to think quickly to give him the best answer as Daddy loved to be always in control and it wasn't the thing to keep secrets from him.

Over the intervening years Charles did try to bring some normality into the family home. His job had provided him with an array of benefits including travel.

Up to this point, life had been a nomadic routine and unexciting. So, Chastity did not hold out much hope for Charles' new idea to inject some happiness into family life. But what did he know about happiness? He never smiled or cracked a joke for he was far too puritanical and clinical. In fact, one would be forgiven for thinking that it was almost sinful to laugh or even smile.

Around the dinner table there was silence. The table was laid with a crisp white lace tablecloth decorated with gold leaf placed strategically in the centre as a central piece which Mummy had purchased from Liberty's on Regent Street. She simply adored it and knew that its presence would evoke compliments from all her guests. It was a special day as it was

Pentecost Sunday or more commonly referred to in Apostolic church circles as the culmination of Easter, a day celebrated which Daddy always respected and honoured more than any other religious day of celebration such as Christmas. It was an exciting day because our cousins who lived in Henley and Cheltenham were coming together with their respective parents, our aunts and uncles who we hadn't seen for a long time. Extended family occasions and get togethers were very rare. Chastity recalled that, as a family they had only met a few of their extended family members. It was not as if we didn't want to meet with them, but that Daddy was rather resentful of them because they had appeared to have fared better than he had, and it was like he was hiding behind this façade thus allowing only the privileged few to really get to know him. But for Chastity this was so unfair because there was a real world out there and she was only being allowed a small glimpse of it. A world away from the stifling environment that was currently home.

11

Peer Trouble

Chastity was constantly being bullied at school. It was something that happened daily. There wasn't just one thing she was being picked on for but a myriad of things. Chastity spoke with a certain accent and her vowels were well rounded. For a black person this was peculiar to her white peers because they still had that imperial attitude about other social groups, never mind those from the western sub-continent. Chastity also came from a family of four when most of her peers and friends alike had smaller families. She was therefore often the butt of many a joke, and being quite reserved and a little shy, she couldn't handle it very well.

Chastity, being quite an affable kind of person with a certain utilitarian approach to life was always considering the wellbeing of others. It came as a bit of a shock then to her mother that she should be singled out by others as a target for fun. Particularly by some of the girls she associated with who had a more cavalier approach to life and were quite lofty in the way they responded to others like they were giving out orders to servants in an aristocratic household.

The teachers were pleasant enough at school but of course, like most teachers, they had their favourites which were usually those who not only worked hard, but who also achieved the best marks in their homework and end of year examinations. Chastity had a good rapport with her English Language teacher who often encouraged her because Chastity always performed well in class and enjoyed the subject immensely. Pupils were streamlined according to their ability and Chastity was in the top stream for this subject, but this did little to stop the perpetuators of the bullying culture who even found an opportunity to target her during the lesson.

Orals formed a regular part of the English Language curriculum, where pupils are given a subject to research and then asked to do a presentation on it. Sometimes, the pupils are given a chance to choose their own subject matter and then asked to do a presentation on their chosen subject. It was a winter's day Friday 16th of November 1979 and the English class had been asked to prepare a timed assignment for the lesson. 'Hi, Lucy,' Chastity called out.… 'Wait for me.' Lucy turned around to see Chastity running up behind her.

'Hello, fancy seeing you here at this time.' It was 8.25am and Chastity was normally in school before then hence the fact that her mother had driven her to school to avoid her being late. It wouldn't do for her to get a late mark. They sauntered up to the cloakroom and locker area before going on to their respective classes. Lucy had chosen different options from Chastity, so they didn't see so much of each other and only shared the same classes for English Language and Maths.

It was 4pm and the last lesson of the day. Chastity stood up as usual as her name was called out to do her presentation. 'Snigger, snigger.' One could hear the troublemakers already sharpening their tongues in the background.

'Quiet,' Ms Brahms said. 'That is enough.' But they weren't to be told. They were the usual culprits. There was Sandra, Lacy-Ann, Stephano, and Deborah. One could be forgiven in thinking that they were pleasant enough but looks can be so deceiving. They had made life for Chastity so miserable to the point that she sometimes did not get involved in discussions in class although she had interesting things to say, just because she knew she would be laughed at or sniggered at. She therefore often remained silent even though class discussions were encouraged.

The girls who engaged in bullying were often referred to as the 'pact' because their reputation preceded them, and everyone knew all there was to know about their misdemeanours. One either joined in with them to avoid being picked on themselves or hated them and did their level best to avoid becoming the target of their bullying, even if it meant joining in with them just to have their acceptance. But Chastity was not of that persuasion. She knew better and preferred to disengage in such unsavoury behaviour. Chastity often wondered if the pact lived such shallow lives that they had to engage in such silly behaviour. It just showed them up in a bad light if they could be so narrow minded as to poke fun in this way.

Chastity completed her presentation amidst the annoying tactics of the pact and opened the floor for questions which was the usual thing to do. She had done so well that that Ms Brahms had asked Chastity to stay behind for a few minutes after the lesson. Lucy wanted to know what Ms Brahms had to say and so waited for Chastity outside. Ms Brahms had good news. A handful of students would be chosen to present their oral presentation to the panel of the examination board. This was a special privilege as only the high achieving pupils were normally chosen to do this. Ms Brahms told Chastity that she was one of the few who had been chosen to present her oral exam in front of the panel. Chastity beamed with pride as Ms Brahms spoke.

'You've done well this year and showed consistent progress. I am pleased and proud to select you to present your oral to the special examination panel.' Chastity reflected on what Ms Brahms was saying and thought that 'Mummy would be so pleased.' Daddy on the other hand, what would he say – nothing much because it wasn't the subject of Mathematics that she was excelling at but English Language. There was just no pleasing him at all!

Chastity left the room on a high and met with Lucy who had been waiting for her.

'So, tell me...............,' Lucy said. 'What did Ms Brahms have to say?'

'Well.......' Chastity started 'She said I was the best ever.'

'Yes, I bet she did,' Lucy said airily.

'No really,' Chastity continued. 'Ms Brahms has selected me to present to a special examination board. But keep this to yourself as I don't want any of the pact finding out otherwise, they will really have a dig at me.' Chastity could trust Lucy with her innermost secrets and knew that Lucy would keep her confidence in this matter.

Three years later....

Chastity completed her secondary education and had chosen to continue her studies at the local sixth form college so she could be near to her mother rather than board away at the college which Lucy had chosen to attend.

12

Teenage Years and Beyond

With her parents, particularly her father, being so austere, Victorian and autocratic, Chastity's ascension into adulthood was fraught with many problems not helped by her many insecurities, self-esteem issues, a self-deprecating attitude and profound disbelief towards others who dare pay her a compliment or comment positively on anything about her. She had already been deemed as ugly by her father and so she wore ugly, she walked ugly, and she portrayed ugly in the way she dressed. It was almost as if she resigned herself to becoming nothing because that was the sentence thrust upon her by her father who had been to date, the most influencing factor in her life. As to boyfriends and no-one was speaking of sexual relations, Chastity lived under the motto 'NO BOYFRIENDS PLEASE - IT IS FORBIDDEN.' Chastity was a principled person. She didn't endorse the concept of casual relationships, one-night stands or anything of that nature. Not that Chastity was advocating casual flirtations that proceeded past the goodbye kiss. She believed male friendships were a crucial part of one's development and progression into adulthood. But to her father, even having a male friend was deemed to be not normal and beyond decadent. To her father it was unwise for girls to engage in friendship with boys even as colleagues. Daddy gave the impression that the rules of engagement when it came to boys was something that had been entrenched in stone and passed down by a higher being. Such views were to remain in place right up to the day he passed on. Chastity had taken the vow of chastity until she married to be sure that the person she was being betrothed to deserved her commitment and love in that he loved her unconditionally and loved her for who she was. Chastity had to make sure any man posing as a potential suitor did not harbour some warped idea in his mind on forcing her into becoming something he desired her to become or try to manipulate her into becoming an image he had created in his mind. Chastity had never been averse in pursuing platonic friendships with boys regardless of what her father had tried to indoctrinate into her as she was quite capable of setting her own boundaries and could say no when the situation demanded it. She believed that any genuine friend of hers would respect her for saying so. In Chastity's eyes and her friend Lucy, who she had confided in, it would appear as if her father were afraid of his children growing up into adults, going off and getting married. If it were ever allowed to happen, although it is almost inconceivable, but Daddy's behaviour was such that if he had his way, his children would be sold as slaves to him and then be released for a fee. He would think for them, speak for them, and moreover, live his life through his children who would involuntary be enslaved to him to carry out and cater to his every whim. But if this scenario was to become reality his children, especially Chastity, would have to surrender her whole life totally in submission to her father and relinquish every ounce of independence, desire or dream she had ever harboured or imagined.

The years up to her seventeenth birthday had been cruel to Chastity. More was to come in the way of challenges, but Chastity was to fight back to reclaim her life with a vengeance but at what cost. Read on and find out..........

Daddy had almost knocked the stuffing out of Chastity, belittling her in everything thing from the subjects she studied, the interests she pursued and the university she eventually went to. He acted like a prat on a whim; it took virtually nothing to set him off. It was like he was so demonized that it would seem almost implausible that he could behave in the way he did to one of his own. It was like he intentionally set out persistently to erode her very existence to the point that life would be no more worth living. It took a lot for Chastity to resist her father's invading force and she was seen as *brassy* if she as much as presented an opinion which was different to her father's, but the reality was that she only was expressing an opinion of which she felt entitled to as a free-thinking individual. It was time for the spell to be broken as she was all grown up and certainly was not going to allow herself to become enslaved to anyone and especially not her father!

Chastity continued to write notes to her diary. Her diary being her closest confidante……. 'Respect and coercion are two different things and although I hold the belief that respect and honour were a parent's rights, such privileges should not involve the manipulating tool of coercion……..' 'Daddy always had to win an argument….' she wrote 24th June… 'Daddy, by his misdemeanours, has yoked me and submerged into this culture of control and I have unwittingly allowed myself to be sucked into this regime and never really challenged but accepted it as my lot. But to break the yoke I need to become frustrated to the point that I thirst above everything else to regain control of my life. I am no longer prepared to live under the shadow of my sister. I need to recognize what's been happening and challenge it. It's like that conversation with Mummy way back when she was significant because Daddy had worked his own spell on his younger daughter Olivia by allowing her to become yoked into a distorted concept of perfection.'

Chastity had enrolled at college and was studying A levels in English Language, Economics and Law. Her English teacher, John Clover was a genial and amiable character and over the ensuing months he had become quite chatty and friendly and always found an opportunity to mentor Chastity whenever she required it. Chastity looked forward to his lessons because he often stayed behind after class to talk with her and find out how she was, addressing any concerns she may have with her studies. One morning, a Tuesday morning, Chastity had the usual double lesson in English Language with John. Chastity had decided to spruce herself up a bit which was a deviation from the rather boring and plain attire she often donned. 'Are you going out after college,' remarked Olivia, 'you look rather nice today.'

'No, I just thought I'd make an effort, but thank you anyway.' Smiling to herself as she took one final look in the mirror, she left for college. Perhaps I am on the road to recovery, Olivia paid me a compliment she thought, making a mental note of the same. Her thoughts began to race and she thought about the day ahead and the impending lesson with John. She questioned in her mind; I wonder what Daddy would say if he knew that my English teacher was showing an innocuous interest in me – unhealthy though it may appear? He probably would say that I was going to hell or going down the road to destruction. How on earth did Daddy ever get married and have children!

'Hello Chastity, ooooooooooh, who are you meeting today, you're looking rather glamorous?' said Madelaine. Madelaine was a pretty girl who had become a close friend of Chastity – in Chastity's perception of things. They enjoyed playing tennis together and studying together after lectures. Chastity hoped that she and Madeline would cement their friendship so that they would remain friends forever. Then one fateful day their friendship ended abruptly.

Chastity had been brought up to believe in God and had attended church at least once a week. She wasn't really committed to her faith but attended church because it provided refuge from the mess she knew as home life. Every role that she had been asked to commit to she had performed with aplomb, and she had gained great respect from her church leaders. Significantly, she had carved out a place in the hearts of the more senior members of the church to whom she looked up to and appreciated their fatherly advice. Chastity had tried to introduce Madeline to church but she had not seemed all that keen on the idea and anyway, she had a boyfriend, something which she knew would be out of place with the expectations and principles of the church which Chastity attended. Madeline was too free spirited in her own words to conform to such ridged principles and guarded her freedom fiercely. Madeline looked the part, dressed the part, articulated well and seemed to have made all the right connections. Surely, she would go far in life Chastity thought.

On Monday Chastity attended English classes as usual and noted that

Madeline looked a bit sickly which was more prominent due to her pale features and freckles. Her red hair was brushed beautifully without a strand out of place. But for her well-groomed appearance, all could be thought to be well, yet still, Madeline looked peaky. Chastity ambled over to the coffee area. 'You don't look your usual self. Is everything alright with you?' And then she noticed having come in closer to Madeline that she appeared to have put on a little weight. Madeline had been an ideal size ten with legs that went on forever.... thereby garnering a lot of attention from boys of a similar age. She appeared to handle the attention well, Chastity thought. She had a figure any young lady would love to have even if it meant dieting to achieve it. Despite her many admirers, she was still approachable and genuine in her manner.

'I'm pregnant,' Madeline blurted out.

'Pregnant?' Chastity gasped. 'How, what, who.........................,' the words just tumbled out randomly. After a while she managed to compose herself. 'You're pregnant? Oh no, what happened,' Chastity continued.

'What do you mean what happened. Don't be so silly. Really, you don't need me to explain.' Madeline retorted exasperatingly. She expected a little more empathy from Chastity. 'I'm pregnant about three months and yes, I do intend to keep the baby. Toby and I have spoken about it at length.' Chastity stood there agog, just staring. At first all she could say was 'Oh golly gosh.....................!' Her mind was all a flurry trying to take it all in. Her mind raced with all the things that was wrong with the situation currently facing her. Her best friend was pregnant, the friend she wanted to have for keeps. But how could things remain the same now that Madeline was pregnant. Her pregnancy had thrown up all sorts of problems and dilemmas and went against all that the church had taught her and stood for. How would she deal with it? What would happen to her friendship with Madeline? Could it survive? There was at least five minutes of silence, but to Chastity it seemed like longer.

'The lecture starts in ten minutes,' Madeline said. 'Let's grab a coffee and we'll speak later.'

'Later!' There was no later in Chastity's mind. She was facing a dilemma which could not have come at a worse time especially when things were going so swimmingly well. After the lecture ended Chastity made her excuses and left to go home. She had a lot of thinking to do. She knew what her father would say about Madeline and even what her church leaders would say too. Because of the way her father had dominated her life and had quite literally forced his views on her, it was almost logical what the next step would be. She had to pluck up the courage and just do it.

Chastity, on arriving home, retreated to her bedroom and took out her Bible. She felt all grown up about the decision she was about to make. On reflection, it was only later in her life after she had taken back the reins of her own life that she would realize she had abandoned a friend in need, and a person who perhaps would have remained friends for life. What a waste!

If Chastity were to have had conversations with her seventeen-year-old self, she certainly would have felt cheated that she could have allowed her father to have such an intrusive impact on her mind. How she thought and her thinking patterns which she would have realized were not sound and certainly did little to portray the true meaning of Christian values in this situation.

Chastity had found a verse in the Bible that had said 'not to be unequally yoked together with unbelievers.' Madeline was an unbeliever and did not believe in church or going to church although Chastity had asked her several times, eventually given up on pressing her on the subject. By getting pregnant, Madeline had in Chastity's eyes committed the ultimate sin – a child out of wedlock! What could be worse than this? That was it. Chastity had made up her mind and she would tell Madeline when they next met that their friendship must come to an end.

There was a weekend between the next English lecture providing more thinking time for Chastity and perhaps she would wake up and realize it was all a dream and none of this was really happening. The weekend passed all too quickly. Chastity faced Monday morning with trepidation. She believed she knew what she needed to do, but at the same time really enjoyed her friendship with Madeline and didn't really want to sever the link. This was the one person who was genuine towards her and there was the strong potential of a lifelong friendship with someone who she worked well together with and whose company she enjoyed immensely.

Chastity arrived at college. She had been crying most of the weekend and had tried to disguise this with heavy eye makeup. As she entered the cast iron gates of the college, Madeline was just locking her car having arrived moments before she had. What better time than now Chastity thought to approach Madeline. 'Madeline,' she called out. 'Over here,' Chastity beckoned with her hand. Madeline came bounding over, her pregnant belly much on show as she was wearing a fitted top. Chastity looked embarrassed and Madeline sensed that she was.

'No point in hiding it – everyone will soon know about it if they don't already,' Madeline said. 'Anyway, I am well, and my recent scan shows that everything is fine with the baby,' Madeline continued.

'That is good news,' Chastity remarked. Although Chastity bore no ill feelings towards Madeline, she still believed that they could no longer remain friends as this would conflict with her position in church, but also more crucially, taking this stoic stance may perhaps win her some favour with her father. It was a cruel twist of fate that had greeted her recently, what with her about to lose her best friend when things were going so well for her, but she had become entrapped by the doctrinal teachings of the church she attended, and the pressures being applied by her father. She really believed she was doing the right thing. No time like the present Chastity almost said out loud.

'What's that?' Madeline responded. This was the cue for Chastity to say what she had planned to say and be done with.

'I've decided because of the current state you find yourself in that we can no longer be friends.' That was it. Short and sweet and to the point, or so Chastity thought.

'Sorry,' Madeline said. 'Are you telling me that you are breaking up our friendship because I am pregnant? I'm sure Jesus wouldn't have reacted in this way. Are you going to allow what some pastor has told you to ruin our friendship? If so, you're not the person I thought you were. Damn you!' Madeline said.

Both Chastity and Madeline stood there for what seemed like ages just staring at each other with neither of them quite believing what had just transpired between them. Time had passed and they were already too late to get to their English lecture but instead proceeded to walk the length of the car park and into the cafeteria. They were still walking together with neither of them speaking to each other when Mr. Jones the Law lecturer and the Head of Year passed them in the corridor. 'What are you two doing? Don't you have an English lecture this morning?' He stopped short of reprimanding them further because he could see that Madeline appeared, to be quite upset.

It soon transpired that Chastity and Madeline were no longer friends and the news had spread amongst the teaching fraternity. Some of the lecturers who had befriended Chastity were very cross with her for leaving Madeline at a time when she needed her friends to rally around her. They tried to persuade Chastity to re-think her decision to sever all links with Madeline. Indeed, what was she thinking of! Chastity's decision may have lost her friends at the college but had won her favour with Charles her father. But as the reality of that fateful conversation would dawn on Chastity, the turn of events seemed a bit warped not least of all to Chastity.

A few weeks later at an English lecture.........................

The class were seated. John enters the room moments later. 'Hello everybody,' John said looking quickly at Chastity when he spoke trying to conceal a smile that had come across his face as he noted what Chastity was wearing.

The lesson had gone well, extremely well in fact, and John had been pleased with Chastity's homework. He had given her an 'A' star. 'As a class you have done well with the homework, I set you last week. The average mark for the class was B+,' John remarked. You should all do well in the forthcoming exams, but I don't want any one of you becoming complacent. Right, we will finish for the day. Don't forget we have orals in the next session which is on Friday. Class is dismissed.'

After the lesson John had asked Chastity to stay behind and when the last person had left the class, he beckoned her to come forward. Chastity normally sat at the back in most lessons but in this lesson, she had found herself sitting at the front and felt quite confident about doing so. 'Hi Chastity, how are you today? I must say you look rather smart.' It was quite natural for John to speak to Chastity in this way as they had over time developed a friendship and mutual respect.

'I am fine and thank you,' Chastity replied, trying to hide her blushing face. Being painfully shy she would cover her mouth with her hand as she spoke, not that there was anything wrong with her teeth, but it was a habit that she was finding hard to break. Later in life as an adult, Chastity was to realize that in fact she had a lovely smile and people would often comment on why she always covered her mouth when she spoke or laughed. In fact, she had even been approached by a modelling agency purely because they had seen a portrait of her in a photographic display taken whilst at university.

'Chastity,' John said, 'you know you can be relaxed with me and please don't cover your mouth when you speak as you have a beautiful smile and you don't need to hide it.' Chastity blushed again. People hardly ever paid her any compliments and when they did, Chastity thought they only did so to be kind. As far as her parents were concerned, she was the ugly duckling and there was nothing special about her. They were even known to pass comments about her buck teeth; they weren't really bucked at all, they just stuck out slightly. Apparently, she had been told that her eyes resembled those of frog's eyes because she had large eyes but not disproportionably so. But compared with Olivia, they thought that she was quite plain and ordinary looking. Chastity therefore found it hard to accept compliments as she did not believe they were being directed at her. When Chastity had joined John's class in September, it wasn't long before it became apparent to John that although Chastity was intelligent, she had a few issues which he regarded as detrimental to her progress. He had therefore tried to help her. He became her unofficial mentor.

'Let's go to my study room. It's quiet in there and we won't be disturbed. You do have time?' John said questioningly.

'Yes, I don't have another lesson until after lunch.' Chastity was quite nervy with agreeing to go along with John to his study as he was known to have a reputation to ingratiate himself in an amorous way with the students or so rumour would have her believe. But she persisted with the suggestion and somehow managed to settle the doubt in her own mind that John was being genuine in her concerns in wanting to help her. As they walked down the corridor Chastity lagged a little so as not to arouse any suspicion from any of her fellow students that something may or may not be going on. Being self-conscious, Chastity was only too aware of how unkind those who engaged in gossip and tittle-tattle could be, and she did not want this meeting that John had suggested with her to become the subject of any tittle-tattle. Life was hard as it was without adding any other pressure.

Anyway, no-one is going to suspect anything if they saw us together in John's study even though John's posturing could quite create the suggestible idea that something unduly was perhaps taking place. But then we could plead innocence as we're only having a tutorial, Chastity thought. Chastity's thoughts continued racing to convince herself that she was doing the right thing and that nothing untoward was going on here.

Once in his study, John set about making coffee and placed a few biscuits on a plate. 'So, Chastity……… you're doing well with the subject. I've got great expectations of you. However, I've recently heard some disturbing news about what transpired between you and Madeline. I'm a little concerned. Do you want to tell me what happened?'

'I'm glad you think I'm doing well,' said Chastity, eager to please. It was always good to hear comments like these being made by lecturers because they flew in the face of the negatively which greeted her daily from Daddy. 'At least someone believed in her,' Chastity reflected. She perched on the edge of her seat, a little stiffly.

'You seem perturbed; you shouldn't be nervous about meeting with me.'

'Oh, don't go on like so. You sound like you're a psychologist seeing their patient for the first time.' The words came out faster than Chastity could retract them. 'Sorry, I just forgot myself. I'm a little tired – so much going on right now. Let's talk. It is good to talk,' Chastity said.

'Only if you want to and feel comfortable doing so,' John said.

'Yes, that's fine,' said Chastity brightening up a little although she still felt uncomfortable because she did not want to be totally open with her feelings. But John had an inkling that her home life was troubling her and he felt it necessary to talk to her about it as it may help her to become focused on her studies. Chastity thought about what John was asking her. She knew that she was a little vulnerable and therefore did not want to open herself up for John to take advantage of her insecurities and then leave her emotionally bereft. But on the other hand, she respected John and felt that she could trust him.

This was to be the first intense meeting between John and Chastity. John had been observing Chastity for a while and although they've spoken in the past it was on a casual basis and more informal.

John braced himself and sat upright in his chair cup in hand and looked straight at Chastity. 'Let me say first off that you are an excellent student but you come across as very insecure and painfully shy. Socially, you don't appear to be able to interact very well with the other students in your class and this may hinder you specifically when we come to sit the formal group exams. I want you to know that you can come to me anytime you feel like you want to talk,' John said, pausing to allow Chastity to respond. She did not respond at first. John appeared to be quite genuine and so affable. She began to wonder why anyone would want to show her any attention or even take the time to talk to her. Usually, people didn't bother with her - had little time for her. No-one really cared for what she had to say; perhaps she hadn't anything to say that that was worthy of attention. Chastity went into a world of her own trying to make sense of why she was the way she was; why did people treat her the way they did always thinking that she was asking for advice when all she wanted was to talk. Why did people act as if she needed their help whenever she approached them. Was there a sign on her heard that said 'please help me as I cannot help myself?' She recalled pleasant trips abroad, little moments of happiness when she had gone out with her older sister Diana and life had been good for a while. And then it hit her - it had all started to go wrong when Mother had become ill, and Diana had left home. It was all coming back to her, but it was difficult as she had somewhat anaesthetized what remained of those episodes and events in her memory in a bid to blot out such dark episodes.

Meanwhile, John was staring at Chastity, not in a strange way but he had watched as Chastity had retreated into herself and was, if you like, reliving some of the past episodes of her life. 'Are you alright?' John asked. 'Chastity, is everything alright,' John said loudly. His voice seemed to jolt Chastity back into consciousness.

'Oh... Yes... But...' Chastity said in a confused state. She then realized she had drifted back into her thoughts, almost as if she was being hypnotized and had absented herself from the conversation with John. Having regained her composure, she straightened herself. 'Oh, sorry. Where were we? What were you saying, I just got lost in my thoughts?' Chastity said. John was not going to be brushed aside that easily.

'I was trying to establish whether I would be able to assist you further with your studies and if there was anything you wish to talk to me about considering recent events,' John said.

'Oh,' Chastity said. 'I see,' she continued. She was not quite ready to let down her guard but somehow, she could feel that John wanted her to take him into his confidence. But she wasn't ready – not ready at all. All her life she had lived behind a façade which she had perfected to the point that no-one really bothered to challenge her even if it looked like she may have needed support or just someone to take her seriously. 'Well, that's very thoughtful of you. I am coping well with work now. It is useful to know that if I need help you will be on hand to provide it, thank you.' Chastity was so polite and always very clinical. Things were not always black and white but that was the way she preferred things to be especially in front of her peers and friends. She did not let them into her real world for fear of pushing them away. They may never want to be friends with her ever again, so Chastity thought. But nothing could be further from the truth. Here was a man, John, who really wanted to help her. Would Chastity give him a chance? Well, this time, she had let this moment pass; only time would tell if her response to help would always be refuted in a clinical manner.

'OK then,' John said, 'we will call it quits today; don't forget your homework for next week and remember too what we have discussed today.'

'Thank you, John,' Chastity responded politely and with that they parted company.

It was Friday, the last day of the college week and John, Chastity's English teacher had teamed her up with Tom (who she quite liked), to do a class presentation. It was 4pm in the afternoon and Chastity had decided that she and Tom should spend the last hour of the day comparing notes for the presentation and going through their material one more time. She had already mentioned to Daddy that she would not be home before 7pm and anyway Daddy was going out and wouldn't be home until late. Now that Chastity had moved on to college her father had become less rigid with her and had allowed her a little more freedom. She was even allowed to have a part-time job. My, how things had changed - or so it appeared, if only on the surface. Chastity had established in her mind that she really liked Tom. Tom was the perfect gentleman, blond hair with impeccable manners and spoke in a cut glass accent. He pursued exciting hobbies - hobbies which Chastity could only dream about. Sometimes she thought, if only she could have become acquainted with had she been born to different parents or in a different setting. But dreams did not always have a happy ending, and this was one dream that certainly wouldn't materialize. Chastity had wondered how John had known to pair her with Tom. Had he known that she had liked him or had a crush on him? Well done if he had a premonition to this because never in a million years would Chastity had propositioned him on the matter. God forbid! But Chastity had got to know Tom a little as he always said hello and always seemed to have a smile for her. Perhaps he secretly liked her too!

It was 3.50pm and Chastity had arranged with Tom that they would meet in the library in one of the study rooms. These rooms had been designated for project work and so Chastity had ensured that she had booked the room in advance so to avoid any disappointments on the day. She took the short walk to the library across the grass and past the pond, which was a fond meeting place for young lovers on a warm sunny afternoon and spied Tom chatting away with his mate Mikey at the entrance to the library. Chastity did not want Tom to see her, so she discreetly slowed down her pace to avoid clashing into him. Danger out of the way, she sped across to the library, up the stairs and into the study room. There was five minutes to go. She knew Tom would be on time as he was very punctual and thought it a crime to keep anyone waiting. In the meantime, Chastity arranged the chairs around the table so that they would be seated facing each other. This was quite brazen for someone so shy. She supposed that if it became too tense for her, she could as a distraction always open the window and act like she needed some air. Chastity had put lot of thought and detail into ensuring that this meeting would go well. 'Hi Chas,' Tom said as he strolled into the room in the relaxed manner that had become his trademark. He was never rushed and never seemed perturbed by anything. He was always very pleasant.

'Have you done your homework?' Tom asked, while getting his books out of his bag.

'I've prepared the material we need to use on the day and drafted out what I need to say,' Chastity said.

'Good, then we'll get on with it,' Tom said. The meeting went well and both Chastity and Tom were pleased with the progress made. 'Great,' Tom said, 'we seem to work well together. Have a great weekend, see you next week.' Chastity heaved a sigh of relief, happy that the meeting had gone well and felt more secure in herself that perhaps she had a chance with Tom.

Chastity went away from her meeting with Tom, her thoughts on whether she could take up John's offer for counselling, which she thought could help with preparing her for any potential male friendship. She had to weigh up any decisions she needed to make against the backdrop of knowing that her daddy would not approve, especially as John, her English teacher, was from a different planet in Daddy's eyes; he belonged to a foreign species; he was a man!!! He would think we were up to no good. John had offered her counselling which was more than anyone else had done, well, apart from her doctor Chastity thought. She had declined the offer put forward by the doctor because it felt too intrusive and anyway, she wasn't ill or anything and didn't want an entry made on her medical records which may work against her should she need to supply a medical record to any prospective employer in the future. But John's offer was different and perhaps he was being genuine in his offer to help me she thought..........

John had also suggested that Chastity would perhaps like to team up with Tom who was also in her English class for other assignments and project work. He thought the friendship, if it worked, might assist to build

Chastity's confidence which now was almost at rock bottom. She did not think John was suggesting a dalliance with Tom, but to have him as a friend or a study partner. But knowing Daddy's stance on boyfriends, platonic or otherwise, John's idea may not be a good idea. Nevertheless, Chastity thought, it's me that matters now. It's my life and I cannot continue to allow Daddy to dictate how I live my life. I need to forge my own friendships and make my own mistakes and it's worth taking the risk of Daddy being upset if it means my happiness is to be assured.

At home with her thoughts and her diary, Chastity could consider the events of the day. But first for some light entertainment. Downstairs in the lounge, Daddy was watching the television and Mummy was preparing the tea, 'nothing unusual there,' Chastity thought. 'What are we watching, Daddy?' Chastity asked.

'Deer hunting on safari. It's a programme about preserving nature's wildlife,' he replied.

'Mmmm, what time does it finish as there's a programme I want to watch, "Armchair Thriller",' Chastity said.
'It should be over by 7.30pm,' he replied. 'Have you done your homework?' he asked.

'Yes, there wasn't much,' Chastity replied.

'Go and see if your mother would like any help in the kitchen,' Daddy said.

'Oh, I've already done that. Mummy has given me the night off,' Chastity replied. Daddy hated the children watching television unless it was something he considered to be educational, but on the odd occasion he would let them watch other programmes which did not generally fit into that genre. But tonight, he had to concede defeat as Chastity had ticked all the boxes and legitimately had some free time.

'Alright, you win, you can watch television if you like?' he said. Chastity took the remote control from him before he could change his mind. Channel three was showing "Armchair Thriller", a programme which Daddy usually allowed them to watch. Knowing how her daddy was very particular about the content of some of the programmes he allowed the children to watch, Chastity hoped that there would be no intimate scenes during the one-hour programme or Daddy, as he was prone to do, would switch over or ask them to leave the room. The programme passed smoothly for the most part. *A murder had been committed by Judy, the lover of a prominent judge by the name of Coleman who had, over the last 6 months, been trying to win over Judy the artistic director of a television company. He had not suspected her of any wrongdoing, but the police were closing in on her fast. She was so close to clinching the deal in ensuring that they would be lovers together forever. Judy had hatched a plan to bump off Debbie who she considered to be her rival in the love stakes in order that Coleman and her path would be entwined and cemented forever. Coleman, for his part, had become very taken with Judy and was beginning to fall for her charms.* There was just fifteen minutes to go before the end of the programme and the unthinkable happened, well in Daddy's eyes by all accounts anyway. There was a bedroom scene. It started off quite innocently at first, just cosy talking, and then the dimensions changed, and they (Judy and Coleman) began to kiss. 'Oh, is that the time, 9.30pm, it's your bedtime soon,' Daddy said, switching over the channel as he spoke.

'Oh, is that the news?' Daddy continued............. Olivia was already making her way to the door. But then Chastity decided to challenge him, after all, she was almost eighteen years old.

'Oh...... I am still watching that programme and it's almost finished and you've switched it over,' Chastity said.

'It is your bedtime now,' Charles replied without even looking up at Chastity as he spoke. He was not about to be challenged by his daughter and not over something as trivial as the television. Chastity did not want to get embroiled into an argument and left her daddy to continue muttering on about the decadence society was slowly sinking into and the trash that was being shown on television. Oh, how Chastity wished she could have taken her daddy on and challenged his argument but she was too tired and didn't really want to rock the boat that was already rocked, dismantled even!

Sex was never discussed in the house. The children were treated like imbeciles. Even their mother never discussed the simple principles of reproduction. God knows that if it wasn't for the fact that Human Biology was an integral component of the school curriculum, how would we ever know the story behind the birds and the bees, Chastity pondered. Musing within herself, Chastity reflected how her daddy even vetted the books that she read. Even the onset of Chastity's periods passed without ceremony. Mummy did not even take the time to sit and talk about issues like these which Chastity knew her mother would be aware of. Chastity found out about her periods through a routine biology lesson when she was at school. Olivia had an accident at school and discovered she was having a period. As for the rest, Chloe and Mary, who knows if with the passage of time, their mother might decide to impart to them the wisdom of her knowledge.

Retiring to bed, Chastity took out her diary to record some of the poignant events of the day.

'………. Daddy being difficult again, wouldn't let me watch television at first then relented. Then pulled a prudish moment when a bedroom scene interrupted the normal flow of things. Sent me to bed without as much as a goodnight. I did so want to see the end of the programme. Daddy is so closed about the most natural thing in the world. How in the world did we get here? Maybe we landed by shuttle from the stars or from the planets Mars or Pluto?'

'Boys, are they fact or fiction, human or alien? I wonder why my parents have a terse moment whenever the subject matter of procreation is raised? Is there something really wrong with relationships? I need to probe further.......'

Chastity wrote further notes in her diary.

'Had a meeting with Tom. Lovely person, I like him. I wonder if the feeling is mutual. Need to advance forward with this friendship - need to discover the depth if any, that we have. Challenge is the task of getting to know Tom as a person, or stick to the principle of no boys, no matter what. Can I afford to sacrifice either?'

'John an excellent English teacher. He appears to be intuitive - but then I suppose it is obvious - that is, obvious that I am shy, withdrawn, and unsure of myself. I suppose it doesn't take an eminent psychologist to deduce this. Top points to him for attempting to address the problems though.'

'Sex.........mmmmmmmmmm...?? Let's not go there.'

The new week had commenced, and chastity had had time to think about the events of last week and what John had said to her. She had decided to take up his offer and have him counsel her. 'Bye, see you later,' Chastity called out on her way to college.

Walking down the corridor she almost collided with John her English teacher. 'Hi, do you have a minute,' Chastity asked?

'Yes,' John said.

I've been thinking about what you said last week and I would like to proceed,' said Chastity.

'Good, then we can meet this afternoon at 3pm,' John said.

Yes, that's fine. 'OK I'll see you then.'

The counselling session

'I am not very happy at home and there are a lot of issues I'm having to deal with. If I could live my life all over again, I'd jump at the chance to do so.' Chastity proceeded to open to John about what had happened with her mother going into hospital and how her father had become very mean to her and that many times she had contemplated running away from it all. How that an incident with the broken mirror had led to her becoming insecure about her looks at the point of almost hating herself but that she had allowed herself this morning a glance in the mirror, something that she had not done for a long time. Chastity rambled on sometimes, not even pausing for breath as if she had to cleanse herself from the ills of the past. It felt rather cathartic.

'I hear you,' John said sympathetically, 'and I am deeply concerned. You are so bright and you have a lot of potential. I feel the only way forward is for you to start believing in yourself. Do your parents ever say anything positive to you or encourage you?' John asked.

'No,' replied Chastity.

'I will recommend a few books that you can begin to start reading which will help you to re-train your mind about the way you think and what you believe about yourself. It may also challenge your belief systems and help you to understand where they emanate from. We can use this as the basis for our counselling sessions should you decide to continue. I would like to offer you my support and become your mentor if you think this may help you. Please go away and think about it. I will mention it to your Form Tutor if you prefer but I will not disclose what we have discussed today with anyone else,' John said.

After the session had come to an end, Chastity knew that she couldn't look at John in the same way as she did before she had taken him into her confidence. Lectures would prove to be difficult as she had opened herself up and revealed her most inner thoughts in an alarming way. No-one, not even her closet friends knew that much about her, and she closed off certain aspects of her life to protect herself. Chastity had found the whole experience of speaking with John as cathartic but at the same time, it was like someone had taken a valuable part of her persona away from her, the things she had nursed and comforted herself with on many a dark night at home, and alone, although she was never alone. The whole experience left her feeling a little bereft.

13

Reflections

Life was changing for Chastity. She was growing up despite her father's best intentions to hold her back. On reflection, Chastity had noted that her father had metered out the same treatment in certain respects to all his daughters with no exception, but had reserved his most cruel jibes for her.

Chastity had suffered immensely, but things had been different, quite different, for Chloe. Chloe was Charles fourth daughter. She had been born at a difficult time when her mother was at her lowest ebb. But it seemed that with the birth of Chloe, there was perhaps a light at the end of the tunnel. Chloe was a pretty girl, very cute, and brought much love to both parents. It even appeared that her birth might help to seal over the cracks in the marriage of Charles and Rebecca and it looked like there may be a silver lining. But after some time, the cracks started to resurface, and Charles was back to his old ways.

Chloe wanted desperately to be like her sister, Olivia, equal to her in everything. She had to match her step for step and be equal to her in everything, even down to the subjects she studied at school. As time evolved, Chastity would discover that Chloe's consuming desire to emulate her sister Olivia would extend even to the type of person Chloe married and the career she followed. Chastity recalled that there was this continuing need for Chloe to constantly to prove that she was as good as Olivia, a seed which Charles her father had instilled in her. She couldn't be outdone by Chastity. This was evident when Chastity obtained her 'O' level grades in which she had done remarkably well. Instead of offering her congratulations, Chloe took herself away from the celebrations desperate to prove that she could do better than Chastity had done when her time came. It was obvious to Chastity that Chloe's self-worth was tied up in how much success she enjoyed in all aspects of her life. Success at school, college and university; success in her working life, and eventual success in her choice of partner, her marriage, and home life. In fact, Chloe had no self-worth because outside of this cocoon, she had nothing, felt nothing, and defined herself solely by society's rules as to what was considered success. She considered herself a worthier candidate than her sister Chastity to rise to this challenge after all she was just behind Olivia in the scheme of things and scored more points when it came to who was treated the most favourable.

Chloe was certainly a victim of her environment, but no-one could see this; one just couldn't see it because she hid it well. She was adept at showing others how not to be so shallow but a closer inspection on how she conducted her own life showed that she was the real victim and not those she was preaching to. She was prettier than her sister Chastity for a start, or so everyone would have her believe and much more confident and outgoing. That was enough to create the impression that she was this well-rounded person that she tried very hard to present to the outside world. Chloe always had advice for others but wasn't very good at taking advice from others. She thought she didn't need it and especially from her sister Chastity. But this confident image wasn't natural to her as Chastity would discover. She had to invent it and live it convincingly to become this ideal that she so wanted others to believe. But the telltale signs were there. Chastity, despite the shortcoming's others saw in her, was quite intuitive and saw through the pretence. Despite the similarities that Chloe saw or imagined existed between Olivia and herself, she was unable to topple Olivia from her position as favourite daughter. Not for Chloe was the grand parade, the pat on the back, the glowing compliments, but nonetheless, she was popular enough to find favour with her father. One thing about Chloe though was that she outgoing and flirty to boot. She was constantly being lavished with glowing compliments ranging from how pretty she was to how clever she was. It was like she was being paraded around like a gift horse. So, Olivia was born to succeed. Olivia liked to epitomize and desired to live a gilded life cocooned from the very realities that life presented. It therefore became natural for Olivia to live this life as it was just part of her psyche.

Even next to Chloe, Chastity felt ugly, she walked ugly, she dressed ugly, or so she felt. Chastity felt like the ugly duckling singled out of a brood of pretty swans.

Chastity vowed never to be a parent if that is how they turn out, all horrible and selfish, thinking of themselves only and harbouring within a power struggle to succeed whatever it cost, even to the cost of hurting those around you, those you supposedly loved! How life could be so cruel.

'Oh God.....................' Chastity shouted out, letting out a shrill screech as she did so. She had almost forgotten herself; she was alone in a café holding out on that one cup of latte and nursing her thoughts. She had forgotten she had company! But it felt good if only to vent out her emotions and how she felt about her life, her family, those she dearly loved but noted such love was not being reciprocated. A case of unrequited love. Is it possible to be loved and yet not to possess love or be loved? Or to receive love but not know how to give love?

What was it to be beautiful, to be admired and to have friends whose love would remain unchallenged or unbridled? Just like Madeline her ex-friend. Just then Jessica a fellow student from college came in. 'Drinking alone, Chastity?' Jessica asked. 'Can I join you?.'

Chastity gestured with her hand........... 'Yes, come over,' as she pulled out a chair. 'What are you going to have - I'll get it for you,' Chastity volunteered.

'Make mine a cappuccino,' Jessica said.' Jessica sat down with her cappuccino. Now here is a stunner, Chastity thought. Jessica was 5' 8' in height, had a willowy figure and auburn shoulder length hair and her parents were something big in the city. 'She had it all going for her,' Chastity thought! She would have a good start in life, with little or no obstacles. How she admired Jessica and her fabulous figure, but Jessica had always insisted it was down to having good genes. Little did Chastity know that Jessica had been fighting her own insecurities and lack of confidence but knew the right things to say and played the part well. She had been acting for a very long time. She too had challenges of her own but had always learned how to bottle them up and mask them because it was unseemly to display them or even speak about them, this being a sign of weakness. Her life to date had been one of camouflage, hiding the identity that had become Jessica Cotter. Her mother was a model and had married a successful investment banker and they had houses in Milan, St Tropez and Barbados. They were truly minted. Could Chastity really have a friend in Jessica. But as time unfolded, Jessica was to become a true friend and confidante to Chastity beyond her college days.

Chastity had become a forlorn figure at school and then at college always alone, mostly studying alone, even more so that she no longer had Madeline as a close friend. Madeline was really one of a kind. Everyone regarded Chastity as a loner. She sometimes cut a pitiful figure as she walked along the corridor to her lecture or sitting behind the desk in the library. She was studious and hardworking but very much alone. She made friends as easily as she broke them. Breaking up was never her intention but her insecurities caused her to hold her friends at a distance believing that she was never good enough to be their friend or ever clever enough. Hence, her circle of close friends was very sparse indeed!

Chastity was quite striking to look at with large brown eyes, of slim build and medium hair, but no-one really bothered with her. She sometimes caught the attention of boys, but her apparent vulnerability had caused many of them to keep their distance. I suppose that is why she had become withdrawn. But present her with a task of writing a debate or essay, and she would become alive and demonstrate an unquestionable ability of intellect, persuasion, indomitable belief, and clarity. She clearly came into her own. She loved to write, or speak publicly and debate on matters that were of interest to her heart.

Chastity loved her parents dearly, but it was difficult because their love was hardly ever reciprocated. If one didn't measure up to their ideal you were considered as a non-entity, someone without any real value or significance to them. Chastity wondered if deep down her mother harboured any feelings of love towards her or would ever dare to challenge the way her husband spoke to her and treated her. What would it take to stand up to him? It was like history repeating itself. A cycle that would perpetuate if it was continually fed. Surely one of them would desire to break the cycle.

Chastity walked the five minutes from the café to her home. She knew what was on the menu. It was salmon and broccoli with new potatoes - her favourite! At least she had something to look forward to! Perhaps she might even broach the subject with her mother about her childhood. Having started the conversation with Jessica, Chastity thought that she might as well continue the conversation with her mother. After all, I am almost an adult - four months away from her eighteenth birthday she pondered.

Chastity put the key in the door and opened the door with such force she almost fell over. 'Watch out dear,' Rebecca called out, 'what's the hurry?' Chastity had almost fallen over because she was so deep in thought. I'd better chill out for a while otherwise they may think something is up.

Chastity muttered silently. 'Oh, hello Mum, I'm alright. I just tripped over.'

'Okay then dear, when you're ready come and help me lay the table as your Uncle Phillip is coming over to tea.' Uncle Phillip was a friendly and pleasant man who always had time for Chastity. He hardly visited, but when he did, he always brought treats for the girls and always had a hug for Chastity. It was like he had a sixth sense, sensing that all was not hunky dory in the Buchanan household. He never let on, but one knew that he thought deeply.

Punctual as always, Uncle Philip arrived promptly at 6pm. He was a stickler for time perhaps because of the time he had spent in the Navy. His word was his honour, and he rarely let anyone down, as he considered how he would have felt if someone were to let him down.

Seated at the table, Uncle Phillip beamed brightly at everyone, including Chastity. 'My, my,' he remarked,' 'you're all growing up nicely, and well look at Chastity, she is blossoming into a pretty little thing.'

'What Chastity?' Rebecca said, swiftly interrupting in a bid to divert attention away from Chastity. It was not surprising as she had never paid any compliments to Chastity. From there on the conversation moved swiftly onto to the topic of Uncle Philip leaving England. Uncle Phillip was contemplating relocating to Canada. He had developed some strategic business links over the past years within his expanding property investment company and within the Canadian property market. He had subsequently grown quite fond of Canada. 'Anyone wishing to join me?' he said out loud.

'I wouldn't mind,' Chastity said out loud, reeling back at the confidence in her voice. She hadn't meant to voice her thoughts but somehow it just came out.

'We'll have to discuss whether such a move would be right for you,' Daddy retorted. 'You have your education to finish here first and remember, Diana is no longer around and so your mother may need you at home.'

'Need me at home?' Chastity exclaimed! 'I'm almost grown up now and don't intend to stay on at home once I've completed my university education.' There was an almost deathly silence. So, Chastity had a voice after all – and she made sure that evening everyone, included her parents realized this.

Moving swiftly on, Rebecca stood up to clear the plates after the first course and to set the table for the dessert. Uncle Phillip joined her in doing so. 'Well done,' Uncle Philip said encouragingly. 'You need to show them that you're taking back the reins of your life. Remember, you have our details if you need anything, anything at all.'

14

Life Beyond the Family Home

Nineteen years of age and university beckoned for Chastity. Her birthday was early and so this would make one of the eldest in her class at university. Leaving home at last. Chastity, while scurrying around for the ideal place to study, deliberately chose to visit universities that were at least two hours away by train in order that she could justify living away from home.

August 23rd and Chastity's 'A' level results had come through; three B's and a C. She had secured the grades necessary for her to take up the offer at Bristol University. It was just over a month before university commenced, Chastity wrote to her diary. Free at last, free at last. Thank God almighty, I'm free at last!

While Chastity's father would be paying the bulk of her fees and living costs, Chastity wanted money of her own to spend as she liked and so found herself two part time jobs showing that she was industrious as well as committed to having a good time whilst at university.

During the day Chastity worked in her local department store, Exquisite, and in the evenings, she worked as a silver service waitress at the exclusive Tiffany's restaurant which was a mile away from her home. She felt all grown up. She had her own money, held down two responsible jobs and life looked like it was on the up. Meanwhile her preparations for university were gathering pace; what with buying clothes, material and books required for the first term and sorting out her financial arrangements, there was a buzz and excitement at home, well at least between herself and Olivia, who no doubt looked forward to having a bedroom all to herself.

'Chastity,' her father called up to her. It was Sunday evening and Chastity was busy upstairs in her bedroom. 'I need to check something out with you.' Charles had been peering over the papers which needed to be signed and which would seal his daughter's fate for the next three years at university. Chastity bounded downstairs. 'Now, are you sure that Bristol is where you want to complete your academic training?' her father asked as Chastity had received several offers from various universities but had opted for Bristol.

'Yes,' she replied, 'quite sure,' she said in a matter-of-fact kind of way.

It was a hot sunny July and Rebecca had appeared to have recovered well from her early bouts of depression and her life seemed quite balanced. Olivia's 'O' level exam results were due out in two days' time. Dominic was away performing with the London Philharmonic Orchestra in Sweden. Mary and Chloe were spending the week with their Auntie Millie. It was therefore a subdued quiet atmosphere with plenty of time for Chastity to organize herself and secure her contact details with the friends she would be leaving behind, as well as ensure that her two younger siblings, of whom she was fond despite the horrible behaviour towards her, would be able to maintain contact with her by email and hopefully come and stay with her on the odd weekend.

Chastity had saved up and had a healthy bank balance from money earned during the summer vacation. Her mother had suggested spending a weekend away in York to go shopping and to buy clothes and other things to take away with her in October. The penultimate week before October 4th, a week to go and Chastity would be off. Her mother had booked an all-inclusive weekend at the Savoy in York which included health and beauty treatments for both her and Chastity, with a week to go before university.

Chastity had made the grade to go to university, something that her daddy had predicted would be impossible. So, shopping for clothes would be something she would relish with some gusto. Her mother had planned a day at the shops with lunch and then a meal out in the evening and then home. It was going to be something of a late night. She had packed an overnight bag in case it was too late to drive back. Chastity had hoped that it would be too late to drive back so that she could spend some quality time with Mummy.

They were leaving at 8am in the morning and having breakfast on route. It was just Mummy and herself. Chastity thought - it would be fun. It was busy on the motorway Chastity reflected, as Mummy had found herself in the middle of the rush hour. 'We should have left later to avoid the rush hour,' Chastity sighed. She hated being in traffic and could think of countless other things to do than being sandwiched between lorries, trucks and commuters as they made the daily trudge to work. One day it will be me doing this daily, Chastity mused. I don't relish the thought. Perhaps I'll grow up and marry a farmer and become a farmer's wife - then life will be so different, more relaxed perhaps and tranquil. Chastity liked to dream but with the proviso that one day her dreams would become a living reality.

Six months on at university....

Chastity loved university, being far away from home and being able to dictate the pace and content of her own life and not having to challenge her daddy's response with every whim and move she made. Her daddy was not too far away though because he had insisted that she telephoned home every week. What a bore Chastity thought. She had thrown herself fully into university life but found social events difficult to manage. 'Boys, boys and more boys, they're everywhere.' Chastity lamented to Sophia, her friend who was on the same course - Law.

'What do you mean?' Sophia asked. Chastity stopped in her tracks.

'Hold on she thought, no, no, no, I need to leave Daddy and his weird concepts behind. I need to find normality whatever that is. I'm leaving the past and my family behind. Chastity reflected that it would make life a trifle difficult if she didn't at least make the effort to ingratiate with her fellow students as much as possible.

From then on, Chastity began to consciously change her narrative. No more Daddy speak she purposed within herself. Soon, she began to excel in her lectures, attacking them with such gusto she soon proved to be popular with all the lecturers as she made them feel like they were doing a good job. 'You're morphing into a goody two shoes,' Sophia said as she remarked on how well Chastity was doing.

'I wouldn't say so. I'm on a mission to prove that I am more than capable of achieving success. With my history I've got a lot to prove to my parents.' Sophia made no comment. But one thing for sure, she wasn't about to give up on the fun she was having.

'Your problem is that you just don't know how to have fun and to let your hair down. You need to live a little,' Sophia said.

'If only she knew,' Chastity thought. But she wasn't about to spill the beans on her family. No, that part of her life was firmly behind her now, or that is at least what she was trying to convince herself of.

Olivia as expected made the grade to go to university and attended the University of London. Daddy was very proud as she was the top achiever in her school. Everyone who was anyone had to hear about how well Olivia had done. There was even an article in the national paper. No stone would be left unturned. It was an article well worth writing about or so Charles thought.

Olivia went to the University of London, only a train ride from Bristol, and which would give Chastity perhaps the chance to assist her sister Olivia into settling in at university. But being so indifferent towards Chastity, she thought it inconceivable that Olivia would want her to become involved in such an intimate manner.

Chastity was soon to discover a new person in Olivia, a genuine concerned person. They soon became like sisters should be, sharing ideas, planning trips, eating out and just doing sisterly things. The only big difference was that Olivia was more sociable and engaged with boys better than Chastity did. She was the social butterfly and the main feature at every party she attended. Everyone wanted Olivia at their party or social event.

University years and beyond. Time had moved on and Chastity agreed to share a house with Olivia her sister and one of her friends. She had fared better than Chastity had and had gone on to secure a good job. Chastity recalled.

Chastity had proven Daddy wrong. He hated being proven wrong and if he were proven to be wrong, he would find some way to excuse, ridicule or challenge the facts as they presented themselves. Feeling elated about her achievements, Chastity was able to a point to dismiss the negative rhetoric spun by her daddy about her. Her success at university had helped Chastity to challenge the belief systems of her father.

As Chastity settled into a highly paid job, she had hoped to win her father over with her updates of her success as it happened but such events did nothing to challenge what he had already perceived to be her destiny. It was like he was the invisible force behind everything she did in life. Sending her advice when no advice was sought. He believed Chastity should settle for anything because nothing good could possibly come her way, nor he did not expect it to. He even got his wife to embrace this negative concept of Chastity and her sisters and siblings too! Couldn't they see beyond his doctrine? Couldn't they forge their own opinions, or would they rather gloat or bask in the false image of perfection that Daddy had cultivated in himself and then passed down to his children. Chastity reflected.

The problem was further compounded as it was hard for them to distinguish truth from fiction. The lines became so blurred that it proved almost impossible to challenge their belief systems so that any thoughts she had were deemed as opinions and those put forward by others were deemed as facts! What a sad life and Chastity had allowed herself to live by those rules, always admiring the successes of her siblings and neglecting to look at how much she had achieved. And when she did so she would be knocked back by her mother who would make disparaging remarks like, 'stop boasting' when she was only trying to rebuild her confidence and belief systems having had her life source taken from her for so long!

But this was Chastity's time now.

Chastity was caught away in her own thoughts but had come to the most important decision she would ever make in her life. She stood in front of the mirror and, as those who had previously counselled her in the past, addressed herself in the third person with a tape recorder in one hand and staring at herself in the mirror as if she was addressing a group of people at an empowerment lecture. *'Anyone who went through much is destined to amount to much. But you must clothe yourself with determination and become focused and understand that your process is not your end but the beginning of good things to come. Therefore, I know that my end is greater than anything that I may have gone through or experienced. I may have had many regrets, but the future was going to be regret free. I need to break the yoke that binds me to the past.'*

15

Coming of Age

The healing process had begun and there was no reason to turn back now.

All her life Chastity had hated being compared constantly with her other siblings and peers she had grown up with, and there appeared to be almost a covert scheme, or plan, however small, to constantly having to prove herself to her parents and have her life held up in a mirror of surveillance. 'Who were these people anyway she thought? And why should they be judge and juror of my life. I don't owe them anything and what concern is it to them that I prove my worth. Life is not just one game or lottery with just the odd few winning the prize of life. Life is a myriad of journeys; some short, some ever so long; some journeys challenging, and some with highs and very lows. At what point could it be determined that I had failed at life? How can one ever fail at life? Is there some known method that determines this? Pray someone show me! Some scale the pinnacle of success at a relatively early age, whereas others, the majority, of which group I belong to, attain to this glorious post after facing three or five major fights in the boxing ring with the scars to prove it, having failed miserably but retained the gall and stoicism to get up and continue fighting.'

Chastity was slowly unravelling the convoluted web which appeared to have been intricately woven around her life. She had harboured feelings that maybe she was cursed, or perhaps someone having a vendetta against her and had somehow spoken an unbreakable bond on my life. But she soon dismissed this notion deciding that she did not believe in all that mumbo jumbo. However, the question remained in her mind as if it was set in stone. 'Why had I not scaled the pinnacle of my potential and achieved all that I had set myself, dreamt about and planned. I thought all dreams had happy endings, but perhaps I have been misguided.'

No, the key to my success lay in recognizing my identity. Who I really am. What makes me tick. What challenges I enjoy, and does it take the support of others to make my dreams come true and for me to find real contentment? I am the one who controls the pace of my life and to be in the driving seat.

There was something soothing and healing about reflecting in this way Chastity thought; rather cathartic. She indulged herself a little more with her thoughts.

'Daddy had failed miserably as a father and had worked tirelessly to keep alive his perverted contorted twisted dream of the life he had always dreamed of having and which somehow, he tried to live out in his children. Daddy had lots of baggage but had failed to see where the root of all his problems stemmed. In fact, he regarded himself as someone who was well balanced. But to everyone else outside his own bubble, Daddy was truly a victim of the trauma experienced from his childhood, the demons of insecurity, low self-esteem which still plagued him, and he was still by all accounts fighting to free himself from his past.

Daddy had single-handedly manipulated Olivia against Chastity so that she could become his sole focus. He had ostracized and abandoned Diana by booting her out of the family home at an age when I needed her most, leaving me totally bereft. Diana was the only with the temerity and confidence to stand by me when others around me left me at the mercy of my father's bullying behaviour. Because of his distorted picture about life and his numerous misconceptions about the value of life and the myths about what defined beauty, he had confined Chastity to a life of hell and isolation while grooming Olivia for a life of success! But deep down, within the core of her soul, Chastity knew - she was that guy in the Bible; yes, the guy who no-one bothered about, leaving him to tend sheep in the field; yes David; he had a destiny - did he not become King though he had been written off as unsuitable and not anyone that should be considered. But Chastity would bounce back - a diamond in the rough - waiting for her opportunity to shine - not to prove to them that I was somebody, but to give others the benefit of my experiences and take my place in society as a restorer of the breach, offering liberty to those who had been held in bondage to the envy and jealousy of others. A restorer to those who had been mentally and emotionally bruised and left without any hope of a life. Children need to be nurtured into becoming adaptable, sociable, and contributing adults and not subjected to being manipulated into becoming something etched in the minds of their parents or guardians. My natural abilities had been somewhat suppressed as I had tried to be someone, just to gain Daddy's love and have a peaceful life - but what of the toll that to date had been made on my life?

And then when I decided to take a different career direction and make my own choices, I was faced initially with a wall of silence, of dissenting commentary, because I dared to challenge the precepts of someone who thought that he was untouchable and indispensable. Some of us escaped and were able to thrive beyond, and others were less fortunate and still bear some of the scars.'

I digress.

Chastity needed to find a place she could call home. A place of habitation; a place of settlement where she could live by her own rules, do her own thing and basically be sublimely happy as who she was. Such thoughts permeated her mind daily. But where was home? Was it working as a sub-editor for the local paper, a job she had incidentally held for about three years? The job offered very little hope for scope or advancement and currently the paper was the subject of a takeover bid which could mean the loss of jobs. She quite fancied herself as a television anchorwoman, fronting perhaps a magazine programme with debates on topical issues or an investigative journalistic programme. Or was home, her place of contentment, being able to travel around the world on a whim without giving notice to anyone because as an unmarried woman, I had the freedom to please myself when and to where I travelled. She loved flying and enjoyed the experience of travelling to exotic and far-flung places, discovering the various cultures that the world offered and living it up in five-star hotels and then returning home to an empty house. But was this home? Would any of these things offer her complete contentment. Maybe I need someone to share my life with. A companion perhaps, no, a husband. Someone to have and to hold from this day and forever. Was this true. Could this really be my reality?

Writing in this manner proved to be soothing for Chastity as she struggled within herself to free the spirit of her soul to assert her identity and find the place in her life she called home; a place of focus and freedom; a place she could compose her own dreams and see them fulfilled.

Having borne her whole soul to her diary and relieved herself of the pain that she had carried around like a heavy weight, Chastity decided that she had to do one thing. And that one thing was to become a socialite, not exactly in the same way as the better-known socialites but start frequenting the up-market party scenes and dining out more often, perhaps paying the upper crust Belvederes Restaurant in Knightsbridge a visit. After all, many of her colleagues referred to her as the eligible young lady, extremely attractive with the world at her feet, a concept she was warming to, and often wondered why she remained unmarried or unattached. Indeed, many had tried to ingratiate themselves with her company and had been enamoured with her classic beauty and style, only for any slight hope of a relationship forming to fizzle out like flat lemonade almost from the outset. At social events, there would be oh so many admirers, but because Chastity was not one to allow herself to relax within the ambience of the environment and allow others to get to know the real her, any chance of romance was snuffed out before an opportunity had even presented itself.

Armed with a new determination Chastity set about changing, if just one aspect, to the routine of her life. She bought herself a little black book so she could keep a diary of her new friends contact details and those all-important telephone numbers for theatre and restaurant reservations.

It was the height of summer and the month of July was proving to be quite a scorcher. Chastity had decided to enlist the help of a work colleague, Rosella in her plans. Rosella was a confident soul and was often deemed to be the life and soul of a party but not in a gaudy way. Her presence at any party was graceful and she had the most impeccable of manners and was extremely socially adept.

'Rosella,' Chastity said as she chatted on the telephone to her, 'I am planning an evening out next week to Belvederes in Knightsbridge, do say you will come.'

'Belvederes,' exclaimed Rosella, 'what's the occasion?'

'Does there have to be an occasion? It's proving to be a lovely summer and we haven't been out much lately. Why don't you come round for coffee and we'll talk,' Chastity said.

'Ok, I'm free this afternoon, 4pm be okay with you?' Rosella asked. 'Yes, that's fine, I'll see you then,' Chastity said cheerfully, hopeful that Rosella would be won over to the idea after Chastity had explained her intentions. Since Rosella was not coming until 4pm, there was just time to do a little food shopping for a light tea and scoot around the shops, if possible, to source other options for the evening at Belvederes.

Belvederes was a fine place buzzing with posh totty, a term Rosella often used, and which served fine Italian cuisine to which Chastity was quite partial. There was often a classical stringed quartet which played softly in the background as diners enjoyed the service. The restaurant was in the central hub of Knightsbridge near Montpelier Street and the service was the epitome of excellence. It wasn't odd to see politicians from either of the main political parties and television celebrities frequenting the restaurant. If you wanted service and class, this was the place to be seen at and to visit.

It was 1pm and Chastity prepared to go out even for two hours. There was just enough time to pick up some bits for tea and to try on a few outfits, Chastity thought. She decided to take the underground to Sloane Square. She loved Sloane Square with its exquisite array of shops, it wasn't busy and crowded like Bond Street and attracted a different clientele of shoppers. The tube stopped at Sloane Square and Chastity got off. She popped into Waitrose and then made her way down the Kings Road and there it was where she had spotted it, Bedales, one of her favourite shops. Bedales was a quaint boutique selling an array of fine ladies clothing from casual attire to suit most discerning tastes, to the odd ball gown, along with shoes, handbags and the like. They only ever had about five of each item in stock which was a good idea as it would almost be impossible to see a whole party of revellers in the same frock. Chastity soon lost herself among the rails of clothes that had been neatly sectioned. A sweet fragrance of jasmine and almond wafted through the air and greeted each discerning customer as they came through the revolving doors. Now this was shopping at its best, Chastity thought.

'Do you require any help, madam?' one of the assistants gestured to her. Elspeth was her name, Chastity noted.

'Not at the moment,' she replied trying hard not to sound irritated. One thing that annoyed her was when sales advisors tried too hard at doing their job. Don't they realize when help is needed, one would only be too glad to ask, Chastity pondered. Anyway, I was enjoying myself until you interrupted my flow of thoughts, she mused to herself. Neatly nestled amongst the other more boring dresses was a shift black dress with a scooped neck. It was about knee length. It had a chiffon underlay over a satin-like material. That would look lovely, Chastity thought, perhaps with pearls or green turquoise accessories. Chastity loved black and nearly always wore black. To her, black never dated, always looked fresh and could be worn anywhere and at any time, casually or for an evening out.

'I would like to try this on, please,' Chastity said approaching the same sales advisor who had spoken to her earlier.

'Yes, this way,' Elspeth replied as she escorted Chastity to the dressing rooms. Even at Bedales, the dressing rooms were exquisite and well decked out with an assistant on hand to attend to your every need. Chastity had still retained her lithe-like figure and looked good in anything she wore, although admittedly she did not always try to dress up all the time as she loved the casual look. But she never wore the grunge look. She had no unsightly bulges or large deposits of tummy fat, after all, she still hadn't had any children, not that she really had a desire for them. The dress looked lovely on as Chastity admired herself in the mirror and she decided to purchase it. I can always return it if I change my mind, Chastity thought.

'Oops, is that the time!' Chastity exclaimed, glancing at the assistant's watch. It was 3.25pm and she had about thirty minutes to get home and prepare tea. Anyway, Rosella was always late; she referred to it as being fashionably late. Chastity hurried out of the store and made her way towards the underground.

Wherever possible, Chastity ate healthy and always made the effort to cook a balanced meal. She had therefore decided on a smoked steak salmon with roasted courgettes, mange tout and peppers with a helping of corn on the cob. She never mixed proteins and carbohydrates together if it could be helped and it was a good thing that Rosella enjoyed the way she cooked so there wouldn't be any fuss when it came to the menu. Chastity had prepared the vegetables and placed the salmon under the grill when the doorbell rang. It was 4.15pm and so it must be Rosella,

Chastity thought. Sure enough, as she peered through the peep hole, it was Rosella.

'Hi there, sweets,' Chastity said as she opened the door to Rosella, 'late as usual,' she chided.

'Well you may have needed the extra time today,' Rosella joked as the aroma of the food wafted through the air as if to greet her.

'Well, I am preparing a little something for tea, something light. You haven't eaten already, have you?' Chastity asked.

'No, I had a light lunch, so tea would be nice, thank you,' Rosella replied. 'So, what's up, something I need to know about?' Rosella joked. 'Got yourself a boyfriend or are you on the prowl?' she jested further. Rosella knew Chastity very well and read her like a book. She was often spot on with her surmising.

'I never go on the prowl,' Chastity retorted.' Oh I give up with you - I can't ever hide anything from you, but I'm not on the prowl and that's for sure. I've decided it is time to extend my social circle by becoming more socially integrated. I'm not counting on securing myself a man, but Lord only knows, a night out is well overdue. So, are you up for it?' replied Chastity.

'Yes, I think it is an excellent idea, but we'll have to invite a few more people, say perhaps three more. What about Philip and my friend William, and perhaps Jessica too. Five is a good number and if you are on the lookout for a male companion, it won't look too conspicuous if there is a group of us,' Rosella responded.

'That sounds good to me. That's settled. Dinner at Belvederes at 7pm next Saturday. I'll leave it to you to inform the others, but I'll mention it to Philip as he lives not too far from me.'

16

Gone Forever................................

Daddy had been a very mean person - what a father. One couldn't help but feel sorry for him. It was perhaps not a position of love for Chastity because her father did not epitomize the ideal father but her love for him was one of sympathy and the desire to minister unto him love or at least the concept of love. He had so missed out on love, the feeling of being loved and the ability to give out love. It was clear in Chastity's mind that her father was where he was at this point in life because of the seeds he had sown and all the regretful things that had characterized his life, whether wittingly or unwittingly. Things he had not said but should have said and things he had not done but should have done. He never once expressed his love in a tangible way but always acted out of duty, embracing a fatherly responsibility to the extent that one was always left with a feeling of indebtedness for whatever he did. What a life to live, Chastity thought.

There is something to be said regarding the concept of sowing and reaping. Daddy was alone, deserted, and one could sense felt isolated and in need of good company. He had become ill and it was thought in the last stages of his life. But he couldn't end his life in this manner; fate couldn't be so cruel. Moreover - what kind of legacy would this be to leave to his children. Mother called to speak to Chastity.

'Chastity, you know Daddy is very poorly, I'm finding it stressful coping with everything. His time is so demanding,' she continued. There is also the pending reality that he hasn't really got much time.'

'What about the support you have from the social services and the ancillary care - does that help?' Chastity asked. Chastity knew from her mother's tone of voice that she wanted her help or some help from the family because at least we would be able to offer her meaningful respite, something which outside help couldn't bridge the gap, however well-intentioned their efforts were.

With the increasing frailty of Daddy, Mummy was becoming quite morbid. For her the way-out would-be death, not that she would ever contemplate taking her own life, but that if she was to pass now that would be the perfect solution. Mummy often spoke about death and the grave calling her home, mused Chastity, as if that was the only viable solution open to her.

Thoughts passed through Chastity's mind daily as she pondered the thought of whether to move back home with Mother until Daddy's time came. Daddy had lived a very successful life business wise. He had made a lot of money, lost a few deals but overall, he was a very wealthy guy. Chastity thought that right now would be a good time for him to invest in the lives of his children by passing down his tips for a successful life, the pitfalls to avoid and generally, just to sit down and talk, something he did very little of. None of his children ever knew what he was thinking about unless it was a subject he felt strongly about, or if he thought that we had offended him or done something which he considered unsavoury. He never really spoke candidly about the things that were important in life like building a family, establishing a good career and life in general. There was always confrontation. Confrontation - Daddy had probably invented the word solely for himself. He did confrontation and arguing very well!

Chastity and Olivia had gone to visit him while he was in hospital. He had spent four months in hospital within the last eight months. On each occasion they had told the family to prepare for the worst case scenario. Their father had multiple organ failure and was virtually being kept alive by a concoction of very strong drugs. He was alive, but just. It was sad to see him like this, yet Chastity still held out a flicker of hope in her mind and she toyed with the idea of taking a photo for a 'before and after picture' to show Daddy for when he got better. 'Get better.' The words sounded so hollow in Chastity's mind as the words resonated in her spirit; it was like even with all the will in the world, this may never happen and the inevitable would soon be a living reality. Chastity and Olivia conversed amongst themselves about a foot away from Daddy's bed in barely a whisper.

'We were so used to seeing him as a robust character, stoic in nature, austere and very much in control of his emotions. Over the past few months, he barely had much to smile about, but then again, he rarely had a smile to share for anyone unless he was completely relaxed which wasn't often,' Chloe remarked.

While in hospital Daddy had more enemies than friends as Chastity had been told by the nursing staff that their father always sought to debate with whoever would listen

Both Chastity and Olivia had a lot of sympathy for Daddy. But nonetheless, Chastity found it hard - because she still yearned for the love that never was, and it was quite apparent daily, that the possibility of securing that love was slowly ebbing away. Chastity was meant to be strong for Daddy so it would be inappropriate for her to now start blubbering away and becoming all emotional. This would not do at all.

Olivia felt like Daddy wanted to talk and open up but this wasn't something he was used to doing and to start now would be nigh impossible. It was getting all too much for Chastity and so she left Olivia to sit with Daddy alone.

Chastity wandered back to the visitors waiting room to reflect. As she sat in quiet contemplation, the tears began to trickle down her face. 'Why had it come to this? She knew death came to us all, but there was so much undone and a lot still left to do,' Chastity pondered. A nurse walked past as Chastity tried to stifle her sobs.

'Are you OK?' she asked.

Not wishing to make a big scene, Chastity replied, 'mmm, yes, I'll be fine.'

'Let me know if you need anything,' the nurse gestured.

'Yes, I will do and thank you,' Chastity replied. She wanted to be alone to think and although the nurse was doing her job, she found her comments unhelpful at this time. The nurse walked on and entered the ward leaving Chastity to reflect and gather her thoughts in peace.

Olivia had returned and it was now Chastity's turn to sit with her Daddy. Olivia looked very composed but the strain of the severity of Daddy's illness showed on her face. 'Alright?' Chastity asked Olivia. Olivia nodded her head in reply. There was no love lost between Olivia and Chastity as although they had had a very strained relationship during their formative years they had come together to present a united front. Although they had put the past behind them it was still evident that Olivia considered Chastity to be inferior to her.

Chastity sat at her father's bedside. 'Daddy,' she whispered, 'it's me. Are you comfortable, do you need anything?' Her daddy looked gaunt; his eyes sad like they were nursing the fragments of a broken dream - in fact many broken dreams...............

There was one thing that her daddy wanted to do and spoke about it often and that was to retire to his place of origin and write his memoirs. 'Who would want to read them?' Chastity thought. No-one really believed that Charles would die in hospital, and so when the family came to visit, they would encourage him to talk about the dreams he still wished to pursue when he got better. On this occasion, things were no different, and Charles opened his heart to Chastity and began to tell her in a slow but punctuated manner some things he had rarely spoken about before. One thing for sure Chastity concluded was that her Daddy had many regrets, things he wished he'd done and decisions he'd made and now regretted. He wasted no time now in expressing them. Daddy had never allowed himself the time to complete his PHD research but now it seemed even more pressing. It didn't matter at the time but now it seemed all too relevant.

'You know Chastity,' he started, 'we have a large family many of whom are leading figures and hold significant roles around the world. We have family members dotted all around the world including Bermuda, Hong Kong and even as far as Delhi in India. I believe my father told me that the family has a link with aristocracy and that somewhere down the family line some of his family members had been Lords and Ladies and one had even held office as an Attorney General.' Chastity listened attentively, feeling rather privileged that her father had chosen to share such private thoughts with her. But she had her reservations because none of these things she was hearing had been proven and Daddy was such a snob, he was probably trying to make out that he was better connected.

Mummy stepped into the room at this junction and interrupted the flow of things. She hadn't been to see Daddy in two days, and she gasped as she caught sight of him, his head just peering out from beneath the sheets. 'Chastity,' she whispered, 'he looks so sickly and weak.'

'But as a family we can still be strong for him,' Chastity said. It wouldn't do to be otherwise, especially as there was some unfinished business to attend to.

'Hello Charles,' Rebecca said, 'and how are you?'

'I'm OK.' His response was typical; staunch as ever, giving little away. This was his usual stance, and one didn't need a crystal ball to predict what his reaction would be. But his eyes told a different story.

Rebecca continued. 'I understand that the hospital has arranged for the aftercare program to commence immediately on your discharge from hospital just like last time. I'm sure that would be good for you. When you're feeling stronger, I will arrange to take you out and we can go along the river walk. It's summer now and the days are warm and long. I'm sure the fresh air will be good for you.' Charles nodded. Chastity wasn't sure if he was taking note of what Mummy was saying to him but nonetheless, it was nice to sit and talk without her Daddy erupting into a debate, confrontation, or an argument. It was like Mummy was in control now. Perhaps now Daddy would take time to listen and learn to appreciate others around him more. For Chastity, it appeared like the roles had been reversed, with Daddy being in the weaker position and Chastity being the stronger one. To her it felt so surreal because Daddy had often tried to intimidate her and was often irreverent. Others had said she had allowed him to do so because she had placed the power of control in his hands, allowing him to determine the outcome of her life. Chastity didn't believe she was beholden to her father anymore, but she did feel that her Daddy had had a negative influence upon her life. But she had started to rebuild her life and no longer felt trapped in an identity that wasn't true to who she was.

To Chastity it felt that she had lived her life in her father's shadow and somehow inadvertently he had imposed his will on her. In a scary way it was like he had almost shaped and determined the outcome of her life to fulfil his desires and ambitions through her. Her siblings and her older brother seemed to have fared better. Most of them they had married and were moving on with their lives. It would appear Chastity thought that up to this point, her daddy had determined how far and how successful Chastity would become. This was perhaps based on his own insecurities and the competitive spirit he had allowed to rule his life and those of his offspring.

Although Chastity had moved away from home and was living in Hampshire, she had remained unmarried and it seemed to her brothers and sisters that she would continue to remain unmarried, perhaps because they thought she did not have the guts to rise to the challenge marriage often presented. Taking her daddy as an example, the very thought of marriage put the fear of God in her, and it wasn't something that she really aspired to do. The idea of marriage was appealing if she could secure the love of a romantic, ideally a tall blond, blue eyed gentleman who would sweep her off her feet and take her away to Italy perhaps and visit the delights of Monte Carlo. In Italy they would set up home by the river and have 1.5 children and possess all the good things that life could offer. But wasn't that the story of fairytales which never mirrored real life? So, Chastity up to now, never allowed herself to dwell too deeply on this topic. But she had been challenged by this picture of marriage and that perhaps this was a shallow picture of marriage - but then one can always dream even if dreams didn't always come true, she had concluded.

Monday May the 15th and Daddy had been discharged from hospital. The doctors had said that he had made enough progress to be allowed home. His condition had been stabilized and the hospital had arranged for a program of after care to commence with immediate effect from discharge. There were amendments that had needed to be done to the family home. These had been done reluctantly because to Daddy, it signalled in a very strong way, that he indeed was sick and things like the home environment had to be altered accordingly. The bathroom had been relocated downstairs and one of the drawing rooms had been converted into a bedroom for Mummy and Daddy. The house was very large, a Victorian house spanning four floors and offered the rapacity for the renovations required.

Chastity had driven up from Hampshire on the Tuesday morning after receiving a tearful call from her mother. Chastity was adept at playing the good Samaritan. It wasn't like she had to put on a façade or be duplicitous in her actions, but that Chastity really had a soft heart and was sometimes a sucker for a sob story. She was also intuitive enough to know when people were being genuine and really needed help, and which she was only too happy to offer.

The roads had been fairly congested as Chastity made her way along the motorway. Perhaps there had been an accident. Despite the chaotic scene on the roads around her, all Chastity could think about was getting to her parents. What was needed was the opportunity to spend quality time with her them.

She couldn't help admiring the beauty of the countryside with the cows grazing in the field and the myriad of buttercup and corn filled fields which littered the scenic mirage as she continued her journey homewards. Yes, indeed there had been an accident earlier, the signs could be clearly seen. There were police cars and two ambulances strewn along one lane inadvertently shunting everyone into the remaining open lanes - hence the reason for the slowing down of traffic.

Chastity arrived at her parents, relieved to have made the journey safely albeit with a few hiccups.

'Hi, Mum, hi Daddy it's Chastity, I'm here.'

'Hello dear, good journey?' Mum enquired.

'Well as good as can be expected.' Mummy directed Chastity upstairs. She had come with her younger sister Olivia. There had been a recent development in that Daddy had become quite depressed and had been refusing to co-operate with the nursing and care staff. Chastity thought that this was to be expected especially as he had been faced with his mortality that death was and is a reality, and that no-one, not even he was exempt from taking this journey.

Daddy looked decidedly pale, and one could see the ravages of death in his eyes. His eyes were very tearful and vacant as if he had been staring out at the passing of an era. Chastity found it very heart wrenching to note how he had deteriorated so rapidly to this degree. He had lost his energy and all hope of recovery. It was like he was giving up on life. He spoke in strained tones gasping for breath as if each one would be his last. All Chastity wanted to do was hug him and tell him all would be well. But that would be like holding out an olive branch and at the same time being unsure of its validation and quality to soothe and bring about healing. The man who had so much and held many in his influence was slowly slipping away from life. Quite alarmingly, being the stubborn man, he was known to be, it was as if he was giving in to his illness having lost the energy to fight on. Chastity was lost for words. She listened as he spoke, sobbing in between sentences and reminiscing about past glories, regretful about the distinct possibility that his dreams for the future would never materialize! Chastity was hard pressed to offer any words of encouragement but tried to lessen the pain by encouraging him to look to the future and not to lose hope. Chastity knew that he loved having his children around him but not in the usual way that most parents would. Daddy needed an audience and someone that he could force his ideas on. Perhaps he had missed his vocation, Chastity pondered through misty eyes.

Monday the 1st of July. It was the beginning of summer for many with long days of glorious sunshine ahead with the bluest skies ever. Chastity loved summer. She had waited all winter to enjoy the heady delights of summer. Sunshine was medicine; what more does one need! This was Chastity's take on it anyway.

Chastity was on a business trip in Edinburgh and was due to stop by her parents. She had just rounded off the last day of business talks with TV executives, a meeting which had gone terribly well and so she had a spring in her step. The telephone rang, it was Mummy. Chastity had not heard from her mother for about two weeks as she had been away on a well-earned break to the Maldives while her Aunty May, Mummy's sister, had come over to help at the family home. Chastity's initial thoughts were that Mother had called to talk about her travels.

'Hi Chastity,' she said. 'Beautiful day, are you at home?' she continued.

'I'm fine Mum. Looks like you've brought the sunshine back with you,' Chastity continued, oblivious to the fact that was trying to interject.

'Listen, dear,' her mum interrupted; and then she dropped the clanger. 'Daddy has passed over,' Mummy said so nonchalantly and in a matter-of-fact manner. Chastity paused before saying anything.

'Daddy gone....'. Her mind racing. 'No, it cannot be.' I needed to be there. Her mother's tone had been so blasé about it, perhaps she was putting on a brave face.

'Chastity,' Mum said after what seemed like ages, 'when can you come over?' But Chastity hadn't responded.

'So, this was it,' Chastity thought, 'the end of a journey, the drama over! This was it. We were at the end of a journey.' 'Yes, Mummy, I'm coming over,' Chastity said realizing that Mummy was still on the phone. Her thoughts were interrupted again by her mother's still calm voice.

'Are you passing by on your way back home, dear?'

'Of course, Mummy, you don't expect me to go straight home after such news. Have you informed the rest of the family, or would you like me to break the news to them?' Chastity asked.

Cheated in life and cheated in death - the opportunity for Daddy to have a second stab at love gone, lost to those last moments before taking his final breath. Chastity kicked herself for missing out on being there for his final moments. Mother had told her that the body had been taken away in the coroner's vehicle with not as much as a bye - bye. She had been alone at home when he had taken his last breath. How horrendous!

17

The Death of a Rose

The silence in the house was deafening with emotions mixed at the departure of Mr. Buchanan. People had come to pay their respects and there was even a tribute in the Sunday Times. Daddy would have loved that Chastity thought.

Rebecca had taken the death of Charles quite badly, not that he had always been there for her. One thing though, his death had caused the family in particular Diana, to rally together. 'Oh dear,' Rebecca sighed.

'What is it Mother,' Chloe said. She was quite often adept at reading between the lines.

'Well..........,' Rebecca said, 'it is so heart rendering to know that Charles had not even made up with his eldest daughter Diana before his death. He was stoic to the very end! A real trouper.'

The death of Daddy was having a crushing effect on Dominic who revered his father as if he were some sort of a God - a notion however not shared by his siblings. It wasn't as if Dominic had somewhat totally escaped the madness of his father despite having spent most of his youth away at public school. His life had been affected to a certain degree and undoubtedly denied him the opportunity of reaching his full potential. Yet despite all this, Dominic never harboured any ill feelings towards his dad. If he did, they were never voiced. It was the consensus that Dominic hid his true feelings behind that sweet smile that spoke no words but hid a multitude of unspoken thoughts; thoughts that hadn't so far been heard or uttered.

Unlike Dominic, Chastity and the rest of the clan, including Chloe and Olivia had the hindsight to see beyond the unconvincing façade which their father often hid behind. Some saw him as a pitiful specimen of a man who never came to terms with his own mortality and shortcomings, believing instead that he could live forever. He had been a very proud man who could never be wrong, and who had an answer to everything and everyone who dared to stand in his way.

Dominic still lived at home preferring the comforts of the family home and the promise of a cooked hot meal on the table every evening when he was home. Mother's cooking was more preferred than the thought of having to wade through the shops of an evening to select some precooked dinner for one to be heated up in the microwave. Like Chastity, he had yet to find his bride but for now, he had many admirers but was really something of a mummy's boy.

After the death of her father, Chastity decided to stay at the family home for a little while to sort out the estate and tidy up the loose ends and put things in place. By doing so, her mother would be able to continue with life without much disruption. Rebecca had become dependent on Charles after her long illness and was not used to doing a lot of things for herself. It was therefore a matter of her adapting to the changes after the passing of Charles and becoming more independent, so that the transition from having a helpmate to having none would be as smooth as possible.

With the passage of time Chastity found that her intention to stay around for a month had extended to almost three months with her mother holding onto her like gold dust. It was becoming quite unbearable. Having become so used to having her own space and doing her own thing, it was like her personal space was being eroded. Mummy was not very much unlike Charles although she was sweet natured but some of that likeability factor had been tarnished by the dominant character of her deceased husband.

Rebecca had only just got over the death of her husband when Dominic became poorly. He was normally a robust person and in good health. He did not seem to be affected by the normal ills and common cold that was a surety for most people at a given time during the year. Dominic always seemed to be far removed from sickness, so the dramatic events that unfolded regarding Dominic's health somewhat confounded Rebecca.

A year after Charles had died, Dominic fell ill. It didn't appear to be anything too dramatic initially, but as time progressed, he was becoming withdrawn and his symptoms more complex. What had happened to bring this episode of events - one will never know. Chastity loved Dominic. He was so gentle, so forgiving, so genuine kind and thoughtful. As Dominic's condition worsened, Chastity had taken to having a daily dialogue with God. 'I'm sure God wouldn't take away such a beautiful rose when its aroma was so potent it could soothe away the somewhat distasteful strains that had so littered the family home environment.'

Chastity had been on the phone to her mother. Her thoughts were far away. She had moved into a cottage near Anglesey just to get some breathing space and have time alone away from the fraught atmosphere of the family home. Things had become quite strained because the family had received some bad news as Dominic had taken a turn for the worse and the prognosis did not look encouraging. There had been discussions with top consultants and his medical team to discuss the steps forward. Dominic had been admitted over Christmas of 2009 and the signs were not too good. It was the bleakest Christmas ever.

Chastity visited Dominic regularly having decided to stay close by to Mummy as she needed the support and she wanted to be near Dominic. She would have conversations with him about his plans on discharge from hospital. They planned to travel together believing that they would have a second chance to live life differently now their father had passed on. Dreams, hopes, new ventures and horizons beckoned, and Dominic was keen to start all over again. Dominic had slowly started to build his life after his father had passed. Re-establishing old career links, re-connecting with long lost friends; he had even started to have social outgoings with a few of his female friends from school. There was a new Dominic emerging and it was a good sign. But then the sudden relapse in his health gave cause for concern.

Unlike Daddy, the death of Dominic was a slow protracted one with his last moments being lived out in a starchy clinic room with the sound of the various machines bleeping at regular intervals. Every day for two weeks it was the same. 'Beep…………… beep.' The sound echoed around the starchy room. The bleeping of the machines greeted you in the morning and the same bleeping of machinery signalled the end of another day when everyone filed out to go home after visiting time was over. In that clinical setting where Dominic lay connected to a myriad of wires, no one really spoke, not even the nursing staff, and when they did it was only to answer questions or update the family on his progress. It was as if the grim reaper was holding court and held every one present in his grip. Another day was passing and Dominic hadn't spoken or sat up in bed or laughed that oh so congenial laugh, which spoke volumes without even uttering a sound, and which could brighten up even the darkest of days.

The light went out in Dominic's life on the 1st of January 2010.

Though the death of Dominic was not meant to have happened, his death served to provide a turning point in Chastity's life. From that moment on she knew that she had to succeed in life and in the journey that was destined for her. Everything she did from now on was for Dominic, as success for her meant success for Dominic. In her mind, Dominic had left this life too early and someone had to finish his journey for him. Chastity believed that this was her role to complete the journey Dominic had started.

No amount of planning could have prepared the family for the events that had unfolded in that fateful year. For Chastity particularly, she had to develop a coping mechanism which was to serve her in enabling her to proceed with life. If Dominic were still around, he would smile and say well done.

Dominic had a smile that could break the harshest of atmospheres and that could lift the doom and gloom that often pervaded the Buchanan household.

After the funeral and the passing weeks, the tears still flowed and flowed, and the cards kept coming.

Some of the comments read thus -
'A shining light that will never be extinguished..............'

'Another angel in heaven.'

'Words may be few, but the memories will surely last forever...'

'We think about what might have been and then all it takes is a passing shadow as a cloud moves across the sun to remind us of the passing of yesterday and that a new day has begun..........'

'The rose beyond the wall – its passing beyond the other side, its natural beauty no longer to be admired by others; but its fragrance lives on in the lives it has impacted........'

Such was the overwhelmingly love and support for Dominic, a webpage was set up in his honour which contained glowing articles. Others appeared in various newspapers and condolences came from as far as Australia. Truly a wonderful light had been extinguished and how were we ever going to replace him?

In a fitting tribute to Dominic, a memorial fund was set up in honour to assist children with musical promise and ability to have the opportunity they needed to reach their potential. His shadow and earthly presence may have gone but his light and legacy will still live on in the lives of those he has been able to impact through his fund.

Rest in peace Dominic.

18

Marriage Beckons

It was like the death of her daddy heralded in a new chapter in Chastity's life and she could live her life, find her identity without the fear of having it crushed by the dominating force that was once her father.

Chastity had found the impetus to approach life with a new vigour. She had grieved for most of her thirty plus life years of her life for a father who could love her unconditionally; a father who could celebrate her achievements; for a father who would be at her graduation with pride but who never showed up; for a father who she could sit down with and discuss the affairs of the heart; but above all for a father who loved her no matter what she did in life. But now that opportunity had faded away with the passing away of summer. But, whereas summer would return the same time year after year, her father would never return.

Five years later...............

The ugly duckling is now a swan, regal and elegant and with the world at her feet. Life for Chastity had moved on in leaps and bounds. Her career had been progressive, being constantly feted by politicians and leading figures around the world of business to speak and give counsel and wisdom on various matters. Through her work she had been able to help so many people who had had similar experiences to that of her own. Chastity was happy; she was very happy. However, there was always going to be a tinge of sadness as her father had not stayed around to witness her success and Dominic would have been so proud.

With former things forgotten and disappointments confined to the dustcart, a new life was firmly being cemented with her future looking very bright indeed. The past was fast becoming a glimmer in the dark and could never threaten the brightness of the future that lay ahead. Offers of work in television beckoned and there was also the hint of love on the horizon. Chastity had survived but not only survived but finally had become the person that destiny had created and had finally been able to erase what she now termed, as 'the forgotten years.'

July 21, 2012, Chastity's 41st birthday and hasn't time really flown. Chastity had amassed a strong circle of friends with whom she socialized with. Her close friend Jessica from her college days worked as a television presenter and had stayed true to her. She had indeed become her soul mate and someone whom she confided in and held as a close confidant.

Jessica said, 'Look how far you've come! Who would have thought that you would be able to enjoy such happiness despite the horrendous childhood you've had to endure. You're a credit to yourself because you've managed to stay focused and keep in view your end goal.

'Yes, but not without having friends like you around,' Chastity quickly added.

Like Chastity, Jessica also worked in the media but as an editor for a fringe magazine and had bought a small flat in St John's Wood. Her network of friends said she had done well but in her own mind, she knew that she had not even tapped into the wealth of creativity and potential that lay dormant within her. But at least she was happy and life was good. On the birthday front, Jessica had arranged an intimate dinner at the Ritz for Chastity and her closest friends.

'Ringgggg.............. 'Rringggggggggggggggggg,' the telephone sounded in the hallway. Chastity rushed to answer the call. 'Hello Chastity, happy birthday, hope you're looking forward to coming out to dinner tonight, should be fun.' It was Jessica on the other end of the line.

'Yes, I'm truly looking forward to dinner darling, it should be fun. Felicity is joining us along with a few other mutual friends.' Felicity and Chastity were soul mates having met at an editor's luncheon and Felicity was currently working for a fringe magazine but was hoping that Chastity could help with securing new work as she worked in mainstream media. Chastity was only too happy to help.

Chastity's story was gradually being retold time and time again amongst her friends and newly acquired besties. There was even talk of her publishing a book. Felicity, like Chastity's other close friends, had heard how she had triumphed and overcome the insecurities that were her companion as a child. Felicity had greatly admired how Chastity had genuinely committed herself to empowering and assisting others who had similar life stories; helping them out of the mire and wilderness that could engulf the very essence of their lives and their individuality.

'There was no point of return and no playing second fiddle to her sisters anymore. People would have to stand up and take notice; people were already doing so,' Chastity had told Felicity.

She had rediscovered that creative streak that characterized her and had glimmered so promisingly as a youngster. Confident and able she began to stand out from her peers. It was almost like everyone was singing the chorus, 'where had she been hiding?' 'How was it that no-one had discovered her before now?' Now she faced a challenge of a different kind - shunning the publicity that began to surround her wherever she went. Her boss at work had decided that she needed to get a team of supporters who would help in her transition and foray into public life. She would need public relations people, image consultants, the lot!

Reaching her mid-forties, love came knocking and Chastity met Philip, a stockbroker who was genuine and well connected but a man with a heart. They had met at a party, but it was no ordinary party, not any party, but a party organised by Sir Thomas Welling, a wealthy landowner and close friend of Felicity. Philip had been invited by Kendrick, Sir Welling's son who was a work colleague at the same firm law firm Thomas worked at. It was not love at first sight, but Chastity and Thomas shared a common interest in tennis and so the friendship blossomed.

The wedding day…… Chastity had eventually married in July of 2016 burying the memories of her past in a cloud of oblivion. It was the most beautiful picture one could ever imagine. It even made the front page of the most exclusive magazine on the market, Debutante. Who would have thought it! Chastity never sought publicity, but it was like publicity came after her but in a good way. Everyone wanted a piece of her, wanting to know her story and how she made it to forty plus despite the traumas that marred her earlier life. Even her sisters Chloe and Sophia wanted to re-acquaint with her again, but significantly, was it because they admired her many achievements which were hard not to acknowledge or was it because they needed to find a way to absolve their guilt? One will never know.

Chastity Buchanan had now found love in a person who loved her for who she was, warts and all. Chastity had evolved into a creature of beauty and tenacity, but above all, she had found her soul mate who was a person with a heart, someone who could empathize, care, and love unconditionally, all the things that mattered to Chastity. She had found love and could happily define it to anyone who asked.

Love is....................

Let's not begin or we'll never finish the story.

About The Author

Adina Rose Benedict who also writes under her birth name, Jennifer Skyers has published books across both genres, fiction and non-fiction.

You can find other books she has written on Amazon and in a few quaint bookstores dotted around London.

The author is also passionate about enabling and empowering people to discover their purpose and has given lectures on this subject at many events.

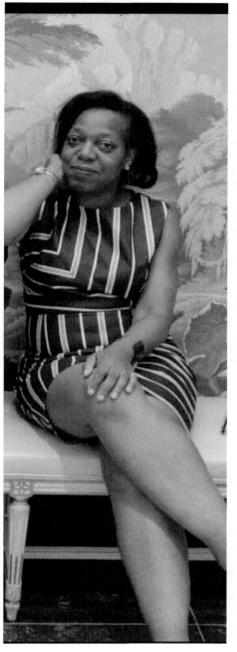

Printed in Great Britain
by Amazon

85347166R00098